An excellent resource for anyone who desires a short and clear guide to Revelation. Alex Stewart focuses attention on the significance of symbolism, repetition and canonical context without getting bogged down in the technical details. Blessed is anyone who reads Revelation with the help of this little book and keeps what is written in it.

—**Külli Tõniste**, President, Baltic Methodist Theological Seminary, Professor of Biblical Studies and Systematic Theology

Without minimizing the challenges of reading and interpreting Revelation, Stewart presents five principles to help readers successfully tour the visions of its twenty-two chapters. While not everyone, including myself, may agree with every interpretive point, Stewart's overall argument is clear and compelling. His engaging style makes the volume eminently readable. Those who read Reading Revelation Rightly will understand better this elusive conclusion to the biblical canon, so I highly recommend it!

—**Mark Wilso**n, Director, Asia Minor Research Center, Antalya, Turkey

Stewart's Reading the Book of Revelation is a must read for anyone just getting started in their studying of the book of Revelation. Stewart makes the book of Revelation accessible to the average reader. Yet, he does so without compromising scholarly insights. The book of Revelation is one of the great treasures of the Scriptures. Unfortunately, most Christians are afraid to set foot in it. Stewart has provided a resource that will help overcome any concerns. Reading the Book of Revelation is exceedingly readable. And the message of the book of Revelation to its first readers and hearers and to us as well comes through loud and cl̶e̶a̶r̶. ̶W̶e̶ ̶a̶r̶e̶ ̶C̶ ̶l̶ st overcome!

w the Lamb:

A Guide to Reading, U f Revelation

Explaining the Book of R r is a daunting task, yet Alexander Stewart excels without sacrificing or trivializing Revelation's foundational theology and message.

—**Brandon D. Smith**, Assistant Professor of Theology & New Testament, Cedarville University

With its scary beasts and apocalyptic judgments, Revelation can be an intimidating book to read. Stewart offers five guiding principles that will lead readers down the well-trodden path of faithful interpretation. Without getting into the weeds of controversy and debate, Stewart illuminates Revelation's main themes demonstrating that John's intention is to motivate his readers to overcome. This book will help you see that Revelation is not primarily about the future, but about how the future makes a difference for us today.

—**Benjamin L. Merkle**, Professor of New Testament and Greek
Southeastern Baptist Theological Seminary, Wake Forest, NC

Fanciful and farfetched interpretations of the Book of Revelation are unfortunately wide-spread and easily accessible. In this book, however, Stewart provides a clear set of principles to guide readers toward a responsible interpretation of Revelation and then demonstrates these through a reading of Revelation that is both consistent in its methodology and charitable toward other major interpretations of the book. Both students and laypeople will benefit from this volume!

—**Dr. Michael Naylor**, Associate Professor of New Testament,
Columbia International University

If you are confused and intimidated by the book of Revelation, whether because of its bizarre imagery or the complicated interpretations it has inspired, this book is for you! Alexander Stewart's five principles of interpretation and his careful reading of the text will give you confidence to read Revelation and guidance to read it sensibly. Even more, his approach recovers Revelation's call for the church to endure faithfully through hardship and temptation until the end - a message we need to hear anew today. I highly recommend reading this book alongside Revelation.

—**Adam Copenhaver**, pastor, Grace Church of Mabton, Mabton, WA

READING THE BOOK OF
REVELATION

READING THE BOOK OF

REVELATION

Five Principles for Interpretation

Alexander E. Stewart

LEXHAM PRESS

Reading the Book of Revelation: Five Principles for Interpretation

Copyright 2021 Alexander E. Stewart

Lexham Press, 1313 Commercial St., Bellingham, WA 98225
LexhamPress.com

Print ISBN 9781683595557
Digital ISBN 9781683595564
Library of Congress Control Number 2021939392

Lexham Editorial: Andrew Sheffield, Kelsey Matthews
Cover Design: George Siler
Typesetting: Justin Marr

CONTENTS

PART 2

The Visions
Seeing Reality

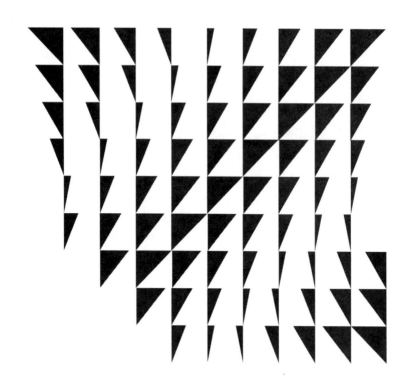

INTRODUCTION

Finding a Way through the Maze

The book of Revelation is often treated as an outcast among the books of the Bible—the family member that everyone else is embarrassed about and wishes would just not come to the canonical reunion. It is not that John is a heretic; he is just plain weird, and that makes everyone who reads his book slightly uncomfortable. How do you convince your friends that your family is normal with such an eccentric uncle? He is always going on about his bizarre visions of a seven-headed dragon, grotesque beasts, and hybrid locust-human-scorpion demonic tormentors being unleashed upon humankind. That is just the beginning; when he really gets going, he won't stop talking about the seven seals, trumpets, and bowls that ravage and destroy the earth and its inhabitants. If it were up to him, your church's children's Christmas pageant would feature a ferocious dragon outside the stable waiting to devour sweet baby Jesus as soon as he was born (Rev 12:4–5). Most Christians consider it best to simply ignore him, especially if you are bringing new friends to the family reunion.

Revelation's strangeness has led to widespread neglect among many Christians throughout history and around the world. These readers have a general sense that the book is probably important, but they prefer to leave it to the experts to figure things out. Such

1

an approach misses out on the riches of the capstone book of the Bible. The main problem is that there are many competing interpretations of this beautiful and rich book, and some of the interpretations are more bizarre than the visions themselves. Ignoring it is certainly the easiest option, but such neglect comes at a cost. There are, of course, some who make the book of Revelation the center of their theology and spend all their time making and revising complicated charts of end-time events. These two extremes are common: ignore Revelation or obsess over it.

Depending on your past experience, it may be hard to think that it is possible to understand and properly interpret Revelation. Such understanding does require effort and study, but nothing valuable comes for free. The first step is to believe that Revelation can be understood well and could become a rich resource for your Christian journey. It could even become a book to enjoy instead of a book to avoid.

There is a successful path through the maze of Revelation's visions. Drawing on sound interpretive practices and the church's tradition of reading Scripture as a whole, this book will consider five rules that can help you navigate the challenges of this complicated-yet-rich book. These principles are the foundational starting point for properly understanding Revelation's visions. A solid foundation makes the whole process of building a new home smoother and ensures that all the walls, floors, and fixtures fit together properly and work as intended. If you have a solid interpretive foundation in place, you will be able to work through the various visions and judge for yourself whether someone's proposed interpretation of a particular vision is terrible, strange but possible, probable, or virtually certain. It is possible to approach these issues with confidence instead of fear or timidity.

The goal of this book is to provide the tools necessary to successfully navigate the maze. These tools will change you from someone who has basically ignored the book of Revelation (or perhaps suffered from overconfident misinterpretations) into someone who understands the book well, can explain it to others, and can reap its personal and spiritual benefits. This book seeks to allow John's distinctive voice in Revelation to be heard instead of being drowned out by the louder voices of the Gospel authors and Paul. To be sure, John's apocalyptic accent makes him harder to understand, and, as with some church choir members, he sometimes seems to be off key (and possibly even tone deaf). Nevertheless, the fact that other biblical authors have stronger and "prettier" voices does not mean that John's (sometimes bizarre to modern ears) apocalyptic voice should be ignored or neglected. Once we are trained to listen well, we will appreciate the harmony; the different New Testament voices are not in competition or conflict. John's first hearers desperately needed to hear the message of Revelation, as do readers almost two thousand years later. We ignore Revelation to our peril.

This book is divided into two parts. Part 1 will discuss the five foundational principles for reading Revelation. These are not an exhaustive or final word about interpreting Revelation, but they are the foundational starting point. Mistakes at this foundational level have misled many readers and continue to breed misunderstanding and confusion today. Now, nothing in relation to Revelation is uncontested, and these points may seem to go against what you have been taught about the book in the past. If so, enjoy the adventure of putting on a new set of glasses for the first time; you may find that they improve your vision. The goal is to hear, understand, and put into practice in the present time what God revealed to his people long ago.

Here are the five foundational interpretive principles:

1. *Focus on the original purpose of the visions.* Revelation is primarily a motivational book, and when this truth is neglected, the whole point of the book is missed.

2. *Let the original historical context guide your interpretation.* Revelation was written for you but not originally to you.

3. *Recognize repetition.* Revelation consists of a series of visions that run roughly parallel to each other; each culminates in the end (Jesus's return and the final judgment).

4. *Recognize symbolism.* John's visions are highly symbolic and need to be read as such.

5. *Read Revelation as Christian Scripture.* This involves using the broader biblical context, especially the Old Testament, to interpret the book.

The five chapters of Part 1 will 1) explain each principle, 2) present arguments and evidence to support the principle, and 3) provide clear and compelling examples of why the principle is necessary or how it helps us understand the meaning of disputed visions. The five chapters in Part 1 draw from examples throughout Revelation. Chapters 6 through 15 in Part 2 will then provide an overview of each of the main visionary sections of Revelation in light of these five principles to show how they work together to make sense of the book. You will come away from this study equipped with a clear understanding of how to apply these five principles to understand the book, how to recognize bad questions, and how to ask and answer better ones. The old saying applies: if you give a man a fish, he can eat for a day, but if you teach him to fish, he can eat for a lifetime. The five principles discussed and illustrated below will teach you to fish for a lifetime.

Finally, there is one more thing required for understanding Revelation, a rule before the other rules, if you will: you must read the book of Revelation. If you have not done so in a while, please stop here and read the book. It is short enough to read through easily in one sitting. Reading the whole book at one time gives you the benefit of seeing the big picture, the whole scope of the book's visions. Such a reading of Revelation will make the rest of this book much more valuable.

PART 1

FIVE PRINCIPLES

Ignore These at Your Peril

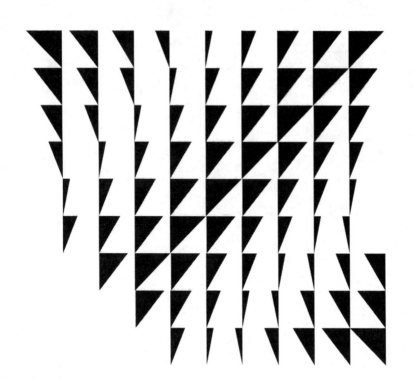

CHAPTER 1

Original Purpose: The Main Thing Is to
Keep the Main Thing the Main Thing

PRINCIPLE #1
FOCUS ON THE ORIGINAL PURPOSE OF THE VISIONS.

I was deeply influenced many years ago through a conversation I had with a pastor. I was eagerly learning all I could about Revelation and trying to unravel its most complicated visions. I asked this pastor about the vision of a thousand years in chapter 20. Did he hold a premillennial, postmillennial, or amillennial position? He bluntly refused to answer the question. He was happy to spend time with me and talk about Revelation, but he refused to answer, even after I repeatedly asked him. He finally explained his reason, and although I can't remember his exact words, his meaning was clear enough: those (and similar) debates have seriously harmed attempts to gain a proper understanding of Revelation because they focus on minor and relatively unimportant issues while missing the real purpose and main point of the book. He was right.

Revelation is neither a complicated book of doctrine nor a detailed timetable of future events. Its primary goal is not to give

9

precise information about events that will unfold right before the end of the world. This is not to say that Revelation does not contain theology or does not describe future events. It certainly does both, but neither is its primary purpose. *Revelation is primarily a book of motivation.*

Revelation fits within the genre of prophecy, but some confusion has crept in here because of different understandings of prophecy. For many people, any mention of prophecy immediately suggests information about the future. This is, of course, sometimes the case. Unfortunately, however, this misses the main point of most biblical prophecy. The Hebrew prophets in the Old Testament do not often give their hearers precise information about the future (although they do that occasionally). They more regularly call their hearers to repentance and faithfulness to their covenant with God to avoid God's judgment and experience his blessing and salvation. John does the same thing.

John's motivational purpose is made evident by an *inclusio* that frames the book, occurring near the beginning and end of John's visions. An *inclusio* is a literary device used to mark off the beginning and ending of a section or entire book by repeating and emphasizing a key phrase or sentence. John employs an *inclusio* in Revelation 1:3 and 22:7.

> Blessed is the one who reads aloud the words of this prophecy, and blessed are those who hear, *and who keep what is written in it*, for the time is near. (Rev 1:3)

> And behold, I am coming soon. Blessed is the one who keeps the words of the prophecy of this book. (Rev 22:7)

This *inclusio* indicates that the words of the book are meant to be kept. How does one *keep* the words of Revelation? Many (most?) discussions and debates about Revelation focus on issues of the rapture, the antichrist, the great tribulation (Are you pre-trib., mid-trib., post-trib.?), the millennium (Are you amil., premil., postmil.?), the number of the beast, and the relationship of the church to Israel, but these debates shed very little light on how to *keep* the words of the book. When these debates become the main focus of attention, somebody is missing the point. Why would someone shine a spotlight on the stagehands rearranging props offstage instead of focusing on the actors actually performing a play? The props are important for setting the scene, but they are not what the play is about. The spotlight should always shine on the center of the action; in our case, we should always spotlight the main purpose of the book.

Keeping indicates action. Revelation was written to provoke and motivate a behavioral response. It was not intended simply to change how we think about certain theological ideas or provide us intellectual information about future events. It was written to change how we live and act in our day-to-day lives.

THE HISTORICAL SITUATION

How does one keep the words of the book? If Revelation is above all a book of motivation, then it is essential to know the goal of the book's motivation. What does Jesus through John want his hearers to do? How does he want us to respond? An answer to these questions requires some understanding of the historical situation of the original hearers.

Several problems confronted the original hearers of Revelation in the seven churches of Western Asia Minor (modern-day Turkey) at the end of the first century, mostly surrounding the issue of persecution and suffering. A Christian named Antipas had recently been killed in Pergamum for his witness to Jesus (Rev 2:13), John had been banished to Patmos (1:9), and John prophetically anticipated a serious escalation of persecution that would surely result in increased hardship, suffering, and martyrdom. In addition, there was growing tension between believing and non-believing Jews in two of the cities addressed by Revelation (2:9; 3:9), and there was internal division among

Christians in some of the churches due to false teaching. John describes these false teachers with metaphorical titles drawn from the Old Testament (the followers of Balaam and Jezebel with her children).

The false teachers apparently advocated compromise and assimilation with the surrounding culture and its idolatry to avoid the social embarrassment of Christianity, evade persecution, and get ahead economically. This is evident because some Christians, notably those in Laodicea and some within Pergamum, Thyatira, and Sardis, experienced little or no persecution. These Christians were affluent and at ease because they compromised and blended in with the surrounding culture (described as eating food sacrificed to idols and participating in sexual immorality—likely figurative for idolatry; 2:14, 20). They were not bearing a distinctive witness to Christ. The historical situation surrounding the original seven churches thus included some Christians who were experiencing difficulty and persecution (tribulation) for their witness to Jesus's kingship and other Christians who avoided the persecution by accommodating and blending in, becoming indistinguishable from the surrounding idolatrous and pagan culture.

It is easy to see parallels between the first and twenty-first centuries. Whether there is real physical persecution or not, Christians who seek to live out their faith are constantly tempted to compromise, blend in with the surrounding culture, and adopt its values (if materialism and the incessant pursuit of short-term pleasure could be called values). We want to live the kind of overcoming lives that characterized God's faithful people of both the Old and New Testaments (powerfully illustrated in Hebrews 11), but we so often settle for a form of easy assimilation that makes life "easier." *The book of Revelation is designed to motivate its hearers to reject compromise and assimilation and embrace sacrificial discipleship.* It thus has a powerful message for our current generation, just as it had a powerful message to its original hearers. Christians must overcome; there is no other option.

OVERCOMING: A PORTRAIT

John's primary goal, in the language of Revelation, is to motivate his hearers to overcome. Every part of the book is designed to transform his hearers into overcomers. For some of his hearers, this encouragement to overcome reinforces their present convictions and conduct, while for others, the encouragement to overcome calls for dramatic changes to their beliefs and actions. For every hearer, John presents overcoming as necessary to participate in God's new creation. One keeps the words of the book of Revelation by overcoming.

Each of the proclamations to the seven churches in Revelation 2–3 ends with a promise to the one who overcomes or conquers (2:7, 11, 17, 26; 3:5, 12, 21). Each of these seven promises is summed up and culminates in John's vision of future life in God's new creation: "The one who conquers will have this heritage, and I will be his God and he will be my son" (21:7). All of the promises about eternal resurrection life in God's new creation are reserved for those who overcome. This is not an optional menu item but the main course. In the middle of the book, John helps us understand how to overcome. Revelation 12:11 states, "And they have conquered [overcome] him by the blood of the Lamb and by the word of their testimony, for they loved not their lives even unto death." God's people overcome by the blood of the Lamb—salvation is only possible because of Jesus's victorious sacrifice—and by their witness. This is not the superficial witness of putting a fish bumper sticker on the back of your car. It is a costly witness that could lead to suffering and possibly even death.

In addition, the book gives several commands that help us understand what it means to overcome. Revelation commands its hearers to remember from where they had fallen (Rev 2:5);

to repent (2:5, 16; 3:3, 19); to do the first works (2:5); to not fear impending suffering (2:10); to be faithful unto death (2:10); to wake up and strengthen what is about to die (3:2); to remember and keep what they had received and heard (3:3); to hold on to what they had (3:11); to buy from Christ gold, white garments, and eye salve (3:18); to fear God, give him glory, and worship him (14:7); to come out from Babylon (18:4); to rejoice over Babylon's judgments (18:20); to praise God (19:5); to rejoice, exult, and give God glory (19:7); and to continue in righteousness and holiness (22:11).

These commands can be boiled down to five main themes: repentance, perseverance, obedience, witness, and worship. These themes occur throughout the book and summarize what it means to overcome. We overcome through persevering in obedience to God's commands, witnessing to God's rule through his Messiah Jesus, and worshiping God for his power, love, and salvation. These things characterize an overcoming life. John is well aware, however, that we are not perfect and that it is easy to fall short in these areas. That is why he also focuses so much on the need for repentance. Whenever we realize that we are falling short through deliberate sin and compromise or accidental drift, we are called to repentance and renewed perseverance.

John does not generally use the language of belief or faith in Revelation. This does not mean that faith is unimportant for John. Faith in Revelation is expressed through the language of witness and worship. When we bear witness, we are demonstrating our

---

Consider the following references if you are interested in exploring these themes further by yourself or in a small-group study.

Repentance: Rev 2:5, 16, 21, 22, 3:3, 19; 9:20, 21; 16:9, 11.

Perseverance: Persevere (Rev 1:9; 2:2, 3, 19; 3:10; 13:10; 14:12), be faithful (1:5; 2:10, 13; 3:14; 17:14), hold fast (2:13, 25; 3:11).

Obedience: Keep the commandments and do good works (Rev 1:3; 2:2, 5, 19, 26; 3:3, 8; 12:17; 14:12–13; 22:7).

Witness: Rev 1:2, 5, 9; 2:13; 3:14; 6:9; 11:1–14; 12:10–12, 17; 19:10; 20:4–6.

Worship: Rev 4:1–11; 5:6–14; 7:9–17; 8:1–5; 11:15–19; 12:10–12; 14:1–5, 7; 15:1–4; 16:1–7; 19:1–8.

faith, and when we worship God, we are proclaiming our faith and allegiance.

The language of victory, overcoming, or conquering (different English words are used in different translations for the same Greek word) is not only used in reference to believers. A scary and ominous picture emerges when the language of victory describes how the beast overcomes and kills believers (11:7; 13:7). John's visions indicate that many Christians would not experience their best life now but would instead suffer financial ruin, poverty, ridicule, suffering, persecution, and even death; the beast would gain the victory over them for a time. Fortunately, that is not the end of John's visions, and it becomes clear that we as Christians gain our ultimate victory by faithful witness in the midst of this suffering. Ironically, we conquer by being conquered.

John draws an explicit parallel here to Jesus and uses the language of victory to describe the cross: the Lamb who was slain is the Lion who conquered (5:5-6). Jesus overcame evil by being overcome and killed by evil on the cross. For John, this should be the normal and expected pattern of victory for Christians. The parallelism is strengthened by Jesus's promise to the overcomers in 3:21: "The one who conquers, I will grant him to sit with me on my throne, as I also conquered and sat down with my Father on his throne." We are called to follow Jesus in his victory by being faithful in the midst of suffering even to the point of death, just as he was.

CONCLUSION

Always focus on the original purpose of the visions. *The book's primary goal is to motivate hearers to overcome. We overcome through genuine repentance, perseverance, obedience, witness, and worship.* John aimed to use whatever means necessary (in this case, apocalyptic visions of judgment and salvation) to motivate his Christian hearers to gain the victory in this life, to overcome. This is the reason he wrote.

This first principle is the most important and least controversial. It is also easily and quickly forgotten or neglected. It is easy to agree with this principle in theory but forget it as soon as the discussion moves to the meaning of the visions and how they do or do not relate to events unfolding on the news. Take this first principle to heart and think about how it changes your approach to the book. Every message and vision in Revelation seeks to motivate you to gain the victory in this life through perseverance, obedience, worship, witness, and, when necessary, repentance.

How many times have you seen this principle come up in discussions of the book of Revelation? It may happen occasionally, but most discussions I have been part of focus on questions that would have likely seemed strange and unimportant to John. With all the other things we will discuss about Revelation in this book, do not let this first principle slip from your mind. Always prioritize the original purpose of the visions. We must overcome, and each of the visions is designed to motivate us to do so.

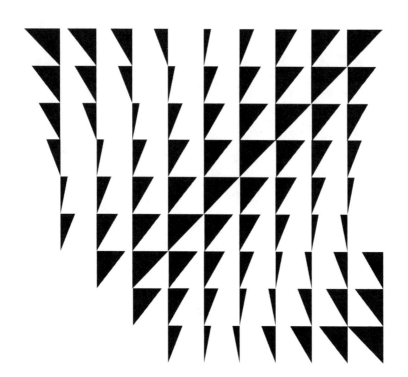

CHAPTER 2

Original Context: The Book Was Not Written Directly to You

PRINCIPLE #2
LET THE ORIGINAL HISTORICAL CONTEXT
GUIDE YOUR INTERPRETATION.

I t is vital to recognize that although the book of Revelation was written *for* you, it was not originally written *to* you. It was written to Christians living in Asia Minor (modern-day Turkey) almost two thousand years ago. The original author and original hearers are incredibly different from us in culture, language, and life experiences. They are like us, however, in the reality of being human; they had the desire for survival, a hope for a better future, and the common experience of faith in God's salvation and promises despite the reality of sickness, death, and misfortune. It is these similarities that enable us to understand ancient people and texts, but we must not ignore or minimize the differences.

Our confidence that God inspired John to write what he saw gives us confidence that Revelation was written *for* us (Paul makes this point in 1 Cor 10:11 and Rom 15:4). It was written to speak to us, to shape our thinking and worldview, and to motivate us to

19

overcoming action—repentance, obedience, perseverance, witness, and worship. Recognizing that it was not written originally and directly *to* us, however, moves us to embrace caution and humility in our interpretation and motivates us to learn as much as we can about the historical situation of the original author and audience. How would they have understood the visions?

This principle helps us properly interpret the book in several ways. If a proposed interpretation of a particular vision would not have made sense or been intelligible to the original hearers, then it is not likely to be correct. This means not that it is necessarily impossible but rather that it is highly unlikely and should be our last interpretive option. The biblical authors, including John, wrote to influence and be understood by their original readers and hearers. Consequently, interpretations that would have made sense and been meaningful to the original hearers should be prioritized.

Interpretations of Revelation that read it as a detailed description of events that would only happen thousands of years in the future make most of the book fairly irrelevant for the first hearers and for every generation of Christians except those living in the final generation. More specifically, interpretations that focus on military, technological (i.e., implanted computer chips), and geopolitical developments in the twenty-first century carry a heavier burden of proof because such interpretations would have been incomprehensible to the original hearers. Much more promising interpretations come from exploring how the first hearers would have understood the visions.

One challenge is that historical information about life in Asia Minor two thousand years ago is not as extensive as we would like. In addition, ancient literary and archeological sources are not self-interpreting. Some take these limitations to indicate that we cannot know anything about the past with certainty, but such skepticism is unwarranted. We may not know things as well as we would like, but enough evidence has survived that we can know many things with a great degree of confidence. We need wisdom to know how much weight to put on historical background information, but we neglect the original historical context to our peril.

THE BEAST AND PLINY THE YOUNGER[1]

With each vision in Revelation, we should first seek to determine its original motivational function—how does the vision work to motivate or persuade me to overcome? Second, we should try to determine, as much as we possibly can, how the original hearers would have understood the vision. For example, in Revelation 12, John receives a vision of a mighty dragon, symbolizing Satan, enraged and trying to destroy Christians, "those who keep the commandments of God and hold to the testimony of Jesus" (12:17). Revelation 13 goes on to describe how the dragon enlists the aid of two helpers or allies, two fierce beasts, in his war against Christians. The first beast is given authority to overcome and kill Christians (13:7). The second beast carries this out by making an image of the beast, which then kills any who do not worship the image of the first beast (13:15).

These chapters become clear when we try to understand them in the way they would have been understood by the first readers. We know exactly how the first readers would have interpreted these two chapters thanks, in part, to the discovery of one letter from among a collection of letters between Pliny the Younger and the emperor Trajan from Pliny's term as governor of Pontus/Bithynia from AD 111 to 113. This is within two decades of the writing of Revelation (around AD 96) and within a geographical area close to the seven churches. The letter is also written by someone (Pliny) who had not read Revelation and did not really care anything about the early Christians. As far as historical evidence goes,

---

1. This discussion of Pliny the Younger is drawn and adapted from Alexander E. Stewart, *Perseverance and Salvation: What the New Testament Teaches about Faith and Works* (Areopagus Critical Christian Issues Series; Gonzalez, FL: Energion, 2018), 29–31.

this is pure gold: an independent source with no hint of literary dependence from a close geographical area within relatively the same time period! Pliny's letter follows. Pay particular attention to the sections in bold.

PLINY THE YOUNGER

Governor of Pontus/Bithynia, AD 111–113

Pliny to the Emperor Trajan

It is my custom to refer all my difficulties to you, Sir, for no one is better able to resolve my doubts and to inform my ignorance.

I have never been present at an examination of Christians. Consequently, I do not know the nature or the extent of the punishments usually meted out to them, nor the grounds for starting an investigation and how far it should be pressed. Nor am I at all sure whether any distinction should be made between them on the grounds of age, or if young people and adults should be treated alike; whether a pardon ought to be granted to anyone retracting his beliefs, or if he has once professed Christianity, he shall gain nothing by renouncing it; and whether it is the mere name of Christian which is punishable, even if innocent of crime, or rather the crimes associated with the name.

For the moment this is the line I have taken with all persons brought before me on the charge of being Christians. I have asked them in person if they are Christians, and if they admit it, I repeat the question a second and third time, with a warning of the punishment awaiting them. If they persist, I order them to be led away for execution; for, whatever the nature of their admission, I am convinced that their stubbornness and unshakeable obstinacy ought not to go unpunished. There have been others similarly fanatical who are Roman citizens. I have entered them on the list of persons to be sent to Rome for trial.

Now that I have begun to deal with this problem, as so often happens, the charges are becoming more widespread and increasing in variety. An anonymous pamphlet has been circulated which contains the names of a number of accused persons. Among these I considered that I should dismiss any who denied that they were or ever had been Christians when they had repeated after me a formula of invocation to the gods **and had made offerings of wine and incense to your statue (which I had ordered to be brought into court for this purpose along with the images of the gods),** and furthermore had reviled the name of Christ: none of which things, I understand, any genuine Christian can be induced to do.

Others, whose names were given to me by an informer, first admitted the charge and then denied it; they said that they had ceased to be Christians two or more years previously, **and some of them even twenty years ago. They all did reverence to your statue and the images of the gods in the same way as the others, and reviled the name of Christ**. They also declared that the sum total of their guilt or error amounted to no more than this: they had met regularly **before dawn on a fixed day** to chant verses alternately among themselves **in honour of Christ as if to a god**, and also to bind themselves by oath, not for any criminal purpose, but to abstain from theft, robbery and adultery, to commit no breach of trust and not to deny a deposit when called upon to restore it. After this ceremony it had been their custom to disperse and reassemble later to take food of an ordinary, harmless kind; but they had in fact given up this practice since my edict, issued on your instructions, which banned all political

societies. This made me decide it was all the more necessary to extract the truth by torture from two slave-women,
whom they call deaconesses. I found nothing but a degen-
erate sort of cult carried to extravagant lengths.

I have therefore postponed any further examination
and hastened to consult you. The question seems to me
to be worthy of your consideration, especially in view
of the number of persons endangered; for a great many
individuals of every age and class, both men and women,
are being brought to trial, and this is likely to continue. It
is not only the towns, but villages and rural districts too
which are infected through contact with this wretched cult.
I think though that it is still possible for it to be checked and
directed to better ends, for there is no doubt that people
have begun to throng the temples which had been almost
entirely deserted for a long time; the sacred rites which had
been allowed to lapse are being performed again, **and flesh
of sacrificial victims is on sale everywhere, though up
till recently scarcely anyone could be found to buy it.**
It is easy to infer from this that a great many people could
be reformed if they were given an opportunity to repent.[2]

There are many interesting details in this letter, but there is only
space to highlight a few here. Pliny writes to ask for Trajan's advice
on the legal prosecution of Christians. He notes that some who
were accused of being Christians "said that they had ceased to be
Christians two or more years previously, and some of them even
twenty years ago." This twenty-year period is significant because
it matches the writing of Revelation to within two or three years.
The persecution or social pressure in Asia Minor during the time of
the writing of Revelation evidently led some to abandon their faith.

---

2. Pliny the Younger, *Letters* 10.96–97 (Radice, LCL).

Pliny explains to Trajan that if someone persistently admitted to being a Christian, "I order them to be led away for execution." On the other hand, "I considered that I should dismiss any who denied that they were or ever had been Christians when they had repeated after me a formula of invocation to the gods and had made offerings of wine and incense to your statue (which I had ordered to be brought into court for this purpose along with the images of the gods), and furthermore had reviled the name of Christ: none of which things, I understand, any genuine Christian can be induced to do."

The choice for these early Christians was clear. If they renounced Christ and worshiped the image of the emperor and the other gods, they would go free, but if they refused out of loyalty to Jesus, they would be killed or tortured (as he later mentions in regard to two deaconesses). This letter anchors the visions of Revelation 12–13 in the historical situation confronting Christians in Asia Minor at the end of the first century. They could worship the image of the beast (the emperor) and live or refuse to worship and be persecuted or killed. This is a choice that has explicitly confronted Christians in various places throughout history.

In the middle of chapter 13, John provides an interpretive comment to directly apply the vision of the dragon and the beasts to his first-century readers (and from there to his readers throughout the centuries). "If anyone has an ear, let him hear: If anyone is to be taken captive, to captivity he goes; If anyone is to be slain with the sword, with the sword must he be slain. *Here is a call for the endurance and faith of the saints*" (13:9–10).

The introductory phrase "if anyone has an ear, let him hear" functions to link these visions concretely back to the proclamations to the seven churches in Revelation 2–3 since each letter ended with an identical call to understand and respond to the message. This vision in chapter 13 not only is applicable to believers living at the last stage of human history but has been applicable to all Christians from the first readers until the present.

John concludes this interpretive interlude by directly applying the vision to his hearers: "Here is a call for the endurance and faith of the saints" (13:10). This is the main point of application for the entire vision of the beast! Interpreters often get into endless debates about the mark and identity of the beast and miss the entire point of the vision. The vision is preparing God's people for the inevitability of suffering, persecution, and death before the return of Christ and calling God's people to persevere until the end.

THE IDENTITY OF THE BEASTS

Following from these historical observations, we can read the texts of Revelation 12–13 with fresh eyes. The dragon, Satan, is seeking to destroy God's people, but he needs help, boots on the ground. He enlists and empowers a beast from the sea (note how chapter 12 ends with the dragon standing on the shore of the sea and 13 begins with the beast coming up from the sea). This beast, in turn, enlists and empowers a second beast from the land to help him deceive the inhabitants of the world and destroy Christians.

John's first hearers would have immediately connected the first beast with Rome and its emperor. In apocalyptic literature, beasts normally symbolize nations (see Daniel 7) and not individuals, so the beast is not likely a single anti-Christ figure. It is also true, however, that nations have rulers, so it is probably not worth arguing about whether the beast should be seen as Rome or the emperor. Rome and its representatives and delegates would have arrived in Asia Minor from the sea in ships, and John's vision describes the beast as coming from the sea.

Furthermore, John describes the beast (Rome/the emperor) as having blasphemous names on its heads (13:1; 17:3) and uttering blasphemous words (13:5–6). Roman imperial coins and provincial coins were in wide circulation throughout the cities of Asia Minor at the end of the first century. Most of these coins had an image of the emperor's head on the front surrounded by abbreviations celebrating the emperor's accomplishments; many of these claims would have been viewed by both Christians and Jews as idolatrous and blasphemous—they completely contradicted what Christians claimed about Jesus.

Figure 1: Provincial Coin, Augustus, RPC 1626

Figure 1 is a provincial coin from Amphipolis (a little northwest of Asia Minor) during the reign of Augustus (31 BC–AD 14).[3] On the front, you will see a portrait of Augustus and can make out some Greek words. To the right of the face, you will see ΚΑΙΣΑΡ (Caesar), and to the left, you can see parts of two words: ΘΕΟΥ ΥΙ[ΟΣ] (son of god). The reverse is an image of the goddess Artemis riding a bull. Subjects of Rome were claiming that the Roman emperor was the son of god, even as Christians proclaimed Jesus to be the only true Son of God.

Figure 2: Roman Imperial Dupondius, Claudius, RIC 56

3. Photo courtesy of the Classical Numismatic Group, Inc. (https://cngcoins.com).

Figure 2 is a Roman imperial coin from the reign of Claudius (AD 41-54).[4] The SC indicates that the value of the bronze coin is guaranteed by the Roman Senate. You can clearly see the inscription: DIVVS AVGVSTVS (Divine Augustus). Claudius was promoting the deification of his famous predecessor to promote himself; he was actively connecting himself to the divine realm.

Figure 3: Roman Imperial Sestertius, Vespasian, RIC 190

Finally, Figure 3 shows a typical Roman Imperial coin featuring the emperor Vespasian surrounded by propaganda.[5] This coin was struck in AD 71, and the text around the image reads: IMP CAES VESPASIAN AVG PM TRP PP COS III. These Latin abbreviations indicate the following: *Imperator* (Emperor), Caesar, Vespasian, Augustus, *Pontifex Maximus* (Greatest Priest), *Tribunicia Potestas* (Tribune of the People), *Pater Patriae* (Father of the Country), and Consul for the third time. The back of this coin is also important because it celebrates the goddess Roma by showing her victorious and powerful; she is holding the goddess victory in her right hand and a spear in her left.

The letter from Pliny the Younger and these common coins illustrate an important historical reality impacting how Revelation would have been understood by John's first hearers: emperor and empire worship. Beginning with Caesar Augustus and increasing

---

4. Photo courtesy of the Classical Numismatic Group, Inc. (https://cngcoins.com).

5. Photo courtesy of the Classical Numismatic Group, Inc. (https://cngcoins.com).

throughout the first century, worship of the emperor and the goddess Roma became increasingly central to daily life in Asia Minor. It became a normal part of being a good citizen and was a test of political loyalty. The cities of Asia Minor competed with each other to flatter the emperor with worship, and emperor worship grew more from the grassroots level than it did from Rome itself.

This helps us understand the second beast in Revelation 13, the beast from the earth. This beast comes not from the sea like the main beast but rather from Asia Minor itself. Its main function is to deceive the people and promote worship of the first beast. This corresponds to local governors (like Pliny the Younger) and rulers in the cities of Asia Minor who did exactly that.

These observations give us a great deal of confidence in thinking that John's first hearers would have connected the first beast with Rome and the second beast with the provincial rulers of Asia Minor. The vision exposes the demonic power and murderous ambition behind Rome's political, religious, military, and economic exploitation of the provinces.

Following our second principle (let the original historical context guide your interpretation), we have a good understanding of how the first hearers would have understood the visions, but does that limit the visions' significance to the first century? Does it say anything about a future antichrist or the great tribulation right before Jesus returns? The answer to both questions is probably no, but that does not mean that the vision is irrelevant to us today. We should answer *no* to those questions based on things we have already mentioned: "beast" in apocalyptic literature normally focuses on a nation and not on an individual antichrist figure, and the time of the beast (forty-two months based on Rev 13:5) parallels the period of time that began with Jesus's resurrection and enthronement as indicated in Revelation 12:6 (see the next chapter). This suggests that the beast is active during the entire period between Jesus's first and second comings.

Certain indications in the vision suggest that even though it symbolized Rome to the first hearers, the beast should be understood as greater than Rome—nations in opposition to God and his people throughout history. Gregory Beale argues for this conclusion and notes that the description of the beast in Revelation 13:1–2 is drawn from all four of Daniel's beasts in Daniel 7:3–8.

> The combination of the four oppressive kingdoms of Daniel into one here does not merely signify the extreme power of first-century Rome but appears to symbolize also the temporal transcendency of the oppressive beast portrayed in v. 2. Just as the four beastly kingdoms in Daniel 7 spanned hundreds of years, so the empire dominant in the first century has latent within itself manifestations of other oppressive kingdoms that may be manifested in the future, as 17:10–11 shows. In the light of Daniel 7, the Roman Empire transcends many centuries and represents all world powers who oppress God's people until the culmination of history. The evil spirit behind Rome will also dominate other world powers which follow it, in the same way that in the OT, the sea beast symbolized not merely oppressing nations but the system of spiritual evil standing behind the nations and manifesting itself in successive world empires spanning hundreds of years.[6]

The vision of the two beasts in Revelation 13 speaks to Christians throughout history as it spoke to the original readers. It does not provide secret information that would only apply to the generation of Christians living right before Jesus returns, but it is rather a message relevant to all Christians at all times. It could be argued that John's divinely inspired visions relate both to ancient Rome and to a specific antichrist figure at the end of time. This, of course,

---

6. G. K. Beale with David H. Campbell, *Revelation: A Shorter Commentary* (Grand Rapids: Eerdmans, 2015), 266.

is possible, but it is not particularly probable since there are no indications in the vision that it would have such double meaning. The original meaning is clear, relevant, and compelling, with no indication that a further meaning should be sought.

CONCLUSION

The book of Revelation was written for you, but it was not written directly to you. Because of this, we should try to discern how the first hearers would have understood the visions. This will help us determine the author's original meaning better than if we were to ignore the original historical context and try to interpret the visions solely from our twenty-first-century perspective. This principle will not solve all your problems because historical knowledge of first century Asia Minor is not particularly widespread, but it will help you identify unlikely interpretations. You do not need to be a historian to recognize interpretations that would only make sense to us today and that would have been unintelligible to first-century hearers. This principle functions to disprove as much as prove.

Instead of looking at lots of visions, this chapter examined a clear and famous example from Revelation 13, the two beasts. There is so much evidence for emperor worship in Asia Minor at the end of the first century that it is possible to claim with confidence that we can know how the first hearers would have understood John's visionary description of two beasts. This starting point is not foolproof but is a much more reliable guide to John's original meaning than trying to identify the beast with the latest global leader or the latest presidential candidate from the opposing party. This second principle does not limit the application of the vision to the first century but better guides us in how to apply the vision to ourselves in the present time. We are part of an ongoing story and find ourselves as participants in an ongoing conflict that has been progressing from John's day to our own.

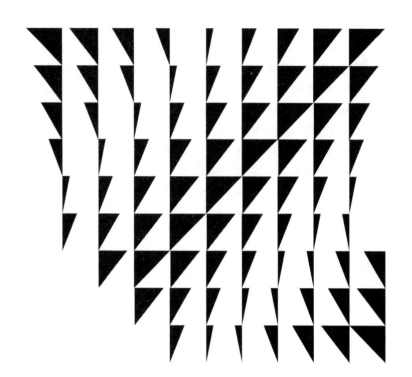

CHAPTER 3

Repetition: Did We Say That Already?

PRINCIPLE #3
RECOGNIZE REPETITION.

The visions in Revelation often repeat themselves. They are not exact replicas, of course, but they cover the same time periods, events, and themes from various perspectives and with different degrees of detail. If you try to read Revelation as a continuous narrative that describes events chronologically or sequentially, you will never be able to make sense of it, and your interpretations will have to be forced and often absurd. Unfortunately, some readers throughout history (many in the past century) have tried to read the visions of the book as a continuous chronological narrative of events that will happen at some distant point in the future right before Jesus returns. This will happen, *then* this will happen, *then* this will happen, and *then* this will happen. Such an approach to the book makes proper interpretation all but impossible.

There is much discussion about the structure of Revelation, and the good news is that we don't have to solve that issue here. We simply need to demonstrate that the visions in Revelation are full of repetition. Once you have been trained to recognize some of the main patterns of repetition, you will be better equipped to understand the visions, and the book will not appear so confusing.

Let's look at some examples to illustrate the point.

WHEN DO WE REACH THE END?

Readers encounter events associated with the end (Jesus's return and the final judgment) many times as the visions unfold in Revelation. This indicates that Revelation is primarily composed of a series of visions that run roughly parallel to each other, and each culminates in the end.

First, readers encounter the end very quickly, in Revelation 6 to be precise. The opening of the sixth seal in 6:12–17 leads to complete cosmic collapse: a great earthquake rocks the earth, the sun becomes black, the moon becomes blood, the stars fall, the sky vanishes or recedes like a scroll being rolled up, and every mountain and island is moved from its place. John describes unbelievers as hiding in terror because "the great day" of the wrath of God and the Lamb had come. "The great day" is a clear reference to the "day of the Lord," the expected future day often referred to in the Hebrew prophets, in which God would act to decisively rescue his people and judge those who reject and oppose him. The cosmic upheaval of this day is pictured by John as universal and final; the reader is brought to the point of no return, and there is no way to undo the damage. We have reached the end. The sun has gone black, the stars have fallen, the sky has been rolled up, and the entire geographical structure of the surface of the earth has been reorganized by a giant earthquake. Later visions in Revelation describe the stars partially going dark (8:12) or falling (8:10; 12:4), the sun partially going dark (8:12; 9:2), the sun increasing in intensity (16:8), the great and final earthquake (8:5; 11:13, 19; 16:18), the sky disappearing (20:11), and mountains and islands being moved (16:20; 20:11). How could any of these things happen later in the book, after they have already happened in 6:12–17? One could argue that the sun only goes dark for a short period, not all the stars fall, the sky moves back into place, and there are four final great earthquakes, but the description of the sixth seal does not suggest any of these possibilities; they must be added to the passage to try to defend a chronological reading of the book as a whole. The fact that we reach the very end in the sixth seal of Revelation 6 is the first indication that John's visions repeat themselves throughout the book.

Second, the seventh seal (Rev 8:1, 3–5) also likely describes events of the end with its mention of silence for half an hour (silence is often associated with judgment in biblical texts[1]) and the casting of fire to the earth, peals of thunder, rumblings, flashes of lightning, and an earthquake. This may not seem very explicit, but the visions of the seven seals, the seven trumpets, and the seven bowls all end with references to sounds, lightning flashes, and earthquakes.

Rev 8:5	Rev 11:19	Rev 16:18
[T]here were peals of thunder, rumblings, flashes of lightning, and an earthquake.	There were flashes of lightning, rumblings, peals of thunder, an earthquake, and heavy hail.	And there were flashes of lightning, rumblings, peals of thunder, and a great earthquake.

The descriptions are not exactly parallel—hail is mentioned in the seventh trumpet, and the description of the earthquake in the seventh bowl is more detailed—but the similarities far outweigh the differences, and each series of seven (seals, trumpets, bowls) seems to bring us to the same end point at the final judgment.

Third, between the sixth and seventh trumpets, John records a vision of a mighty angel.

---

1. Isa 41:1; 47:5; Lam 2:10; 3:28–29; Amos 8:3; Hab 2:20; Zeph 1:7, 11; Zech 2:13; Rom 3:19.

> And the angel whom I saw standing on the sea and on the
> land raised his right hand to heaven and swore by him who
> lives forever and ever, who created heaven and what is in
> it, the earth and what is in it, and the sea and what is in it,
> that *there would be no more delay,* but that *in the days of the*
> *trumpet call to be sounded by the seventh angel, the mystery of*
> *God would be fulfilled,* just as he announced to his servants
> the prophets. (Rev 10:5–7)

The original Greek is a bit blunter: the angel swore that "time
(*chronos*) will be no more" (10:6). The angel is swearing that the
seventh trumpet would be the end and that God's mystery would
finally be fulfilled.

Fourth, the description of the seventh trumpet itself clearly
pictures the end. The seventh trumpet signals that "the kingdom
of the world has become the kingdom of our Lord and of his Christ,
and he shall reign forever and ever" (Rev 11:15). The hymn that
follows celebrates the fact that God has begun to reign and the
time has come for God's wrath, the judgment of the dead, and the
rewarding of God's faithful people (11:18). The phrase describing
God earlier in the book as the one "who is and who was and who
is to come" (1:4, 8; 4:8) is also changed at this point to "who is and
who was" (11:17). He is no longer described as coming in the future
because with the seventh trumpet he came, established his kingdom on earth, and completed the final judgment, with its punishment and rewards.

Fifth, the vision of two harvests describes the final judgment
(Rev 14:14–20). An angel swings his sickle of judgment across the
earth and gathers the grape harvest of humanity for judgment.
The grapes are thrown into "the great winepress of the wrath of
God. And the winepress was trodden outside the city" (14:19–20).
This language is parallel to language used for the judgment associ-
ated with Jesus's return: "He will tread the winepress of the fury of
the wrath of God the Almighty" (19:15). This vision of the harvest

of the earth in Revelation 14 seems to describe a universal final judgment parallel to later visions of judgment.

Sixth, the seventh bowl judgment (Rev 16:17-21) is said to be the end of God's judgments (15:1, 8). With the pouring out of the seventh bowl, a loud voice comes from the temple to declare, "It is done" (16:17). God repeats this phrase when describing the beginning of his new creation in 21:6. The description of the seventh bowl parallels both the sixth seal and the final judgment in the way it describes geographical upheaval.

Rev 6:14	Rev 16:20	Rev 20:11
The sky vanished like a scroll that is being rolled up, and every mountain and island was removed from its place.	And every island fled away, and no mountains were to be found.	Then I saw a great white throne and him who was seated on it. From his presence earth and sky fled away, and no place was found for them.

Does every island and mountain move three different times or only one time during the geographical and cosmic upheaval preceding the final judgment?

Seventh, the final judgment is described for the final time in Revelation 20:11-15. This is the formal description of the great white throne, the book of life, and judgment of those not found in the book of life. Although the earlier visions do not describe God's judgment in exactly the same way, they all make clear that they end at this event. *Revelation is primarily composed of a series of visions that run roughly parallel to each other, and each culminates in events associated with the end (Jesus's return and the final judgment).*

In addition to these seven times the end is explicitly mentioned or reached throughout the book, we can add three more examples. The vision of the two witnesses also concludes with the judgment of an earthquake (Rev 11:13). This is parallel to the endings of the seven seals, trumpets, and bowls and could also indicate that this vision ends with the same event, the final judgment. Additionally, we reach the final judgment in the visions of the final battle and the fall of Babylon, but these will be discussed separately below.

HOW MANY FINAL BATTLES ARE THERE?

John's visions also repeatedly move us up to the end and the judgment immediately preceding it through descriptions of a final battle, war, or conflict. A (final) battle or war is repeatedly mentioned throughout the book. This battle is one that Satan and the beasts wage against God's people and that is decisively won by Jesus at his return.

Rev 11:7	Rev 12:17	Rev 16:14
And when they have finished their testimony, the beast that rises from the bottomless pit *will make war* on them and conquer them and kill them.	Then the dragon became furious with the woman and went off *to make war* on the rest of her offspring, on those who keep the commandments of God and hold to the testimony of Jesus.	For they are demonic spirits, performing signs, who go abroad to the kings of the whole world, *to assemble them for battle* on the great day of God the Almighty.
Rev 17:14	**Rev 19:19**	**Rev 20:8**
They will *make war* on the Lamb, and the Lamb will conquer them, for he is Lord of lords and King of kings, and those with him are called and chosen and faithful.	And I saw the beast and the kings of the earth with their armies *gathered to make war* against him who was sitting on the horse and against his army.	And [Satan] will come out to deceive the nations that are at the four corners of the earth, Gog and Magog, *to gather them for battle*.

The repetition of war or battle in 11:7, 12:17, and 17:14 and the phrase "gather/assemble them together for war" in 16:14, 19:19, and 20:8 should suggest not six different eschatological battles or wars but one ongoing conflict that intensifies and culminates with Jesus's return. If we try to read the book as if the visions build on each other chronologically, then we are left with multiple final battles. Recognizing that John has in mind one final conflict, which is described multiple times in various ways in different visions, clarifies our interpretation immensely and helps us avoid complicated end-time charts that would have made John's head spin.

HOW OFTEN DOES BABYLON FALL?

Similarly, John's visions regularly mention and describe the judgment of Babylon (Rev 14:8; 16:19; 17:16; 18:2, 10, 17, 19–21; 19:2–3). Does Babylon fall two times, three times, five times, or just once in God's final judgment? I suggest that Babylon only falls once, but John describes this fall several different times and ways in multiple visions. The visions do not repeat each other exactly but provide different perspectives and details on God's judgment of the godless economic and religious world system.

IS THERE A SEVEN-YEAR TRIBULATION?

It may come as a surprise to you, but Revelation never mentions a seven-year period of tribulation. John's visions instead mention a three-and-a-half-year period of persecution five different times (11:2 [42 months], 3 [1,260 days]; 12:6 [1,260 days], 12:14 [time, times, and half a time]; 13:5 [42 months]). If we try to read the visions in a chronological way, we get seventeen-and-a-half years of persecution. Nobody argues for a seventeen-and-a-half-year tribulation, so everybody recognizes some repetition in John's visions. I would argue that the different visions that contain this three-and-a-half-year period are roughly parallel to each other, describing the same time period and progression of events from different perspectives and with different details. Chapters 10 and 11 below will discussed this more, but we can make some initial comments at this point.

First, John is most likely drawing this number from Daniel's vision of a three-and-a-half-year period of persecution for God's people in the end times with particular focus on the temple (Dan 7:25; 9:27; 12:7, 11–12). Interpreters have also drawn connections to Elijah's three-and-a-half-year judgment of drought (1 Kgs 18:1; Luke 4:25; Jas 5:17) and the way the Israelites had forty-two encampments during their years in the wilderness (Num 33:5–49; compare the wilderness setting of Rev 12:6, 14).

Second, each vision of three-and-a-half years in Revelation describes a period of persecution during which God's people must bear faithful witness no matter the cost. This period culminates with the end (final battle, Christ's return, and final judgment).

Rev 11:2	Rev 11:3	Rev 12:6
[B]ut do not measure the court outside the temple; leave that out, for it is given over to the nations, and they will trample the holy city for *forty-two months.*	And I will grant authority to my two witnesses, and they will prophesy for *1,260 days,* clothed in sackcloth.	And the woman fled into the wilderness, where she has a place prepared by God, in which she is to be nourished for *1,260 days.*

Rev 12:14	Rev 13:5, 7
But the woman was given the two wings of the great eagle so that she might fly from the serpent into the wilderness, to the place where she is to be nourished for a *time, and times, and half a time.*	And the beast was … allowed to exercise authority for *forty-two months.* … Also it was allowed to make war on the saints and to conquer them.

Third, three-and-a-half years is not a literal time period but is symbolic for a long period of time. This is evident because Revelation 12:5–6 indicates that this period of time began with Jesus's ascension to the right hand of the Father in heaven: "She gave birth to a male child, one who is to rule all the nations with a rod of iron, but her child was caught up to God and to his throne, and the woman fled into the wilderness, where she has a place prepared by God, in which she is to be nourished for 1,260 days." This vision moves quickly from Jesus's birth to his ascension and enthronement in heaven. Without any indication of a chronological break or long period of time, the vision describes the beginning of the 1,260 days. The symbolic three-and-a-half-year period of tribulation began at the point of Jesus's ascension!

This is important because John thus indicates that the visions in Revelation 11–13 cover the period from Jesus's enthronement until his return. His first readers would have recognized themselves as living in this time, and we are living in the same time period today. It is a time of suffering and persecution, during which we must faithfully bear witness to Jesus's lordship and keep his commandments in the face of external persecution and internal temptation to compromise.

This may be a new way of thinking about the end times, but a careful reading of Revelation indicates that *there will be no future literal seven-year period of tribulation before Jesus returns*. Each reference to this three-and-a-half-year period of tribulation is roughly parallel and describes the period of time between Jesus's first and second comings. This observation certainly helps to simplify many of the complicated and confusing charts of the end times you may have come across in your life. Incidentally, this reading of John's visions fits well with broader New Testament theological themes. The early Christians viewed themselves as living in tribulation (Greek: *thlipsis*)[2] and saw the end times as having begun with Jesus's coming and the pouring out of the Holy Spirit.[3] John's visions are perfectly in line with these early Christian convictions.

---

2. On tribulation as a present reality: Matt 13:21; 24:9; Mark 4:17; John 16:33; Acts 11:19; 14:22; 20:23; Rom 5:3; 8:35; 12:12; 2 Cor 1:4, 8; 4:17; 6:4; 8:2; Col 1:24; 1 Thess 1:6; 3:3; 2 Thess 1:4; Heb 10:33; Rev 1:9; 2:9, 10.

3. On living in the end times: Mark 1:15; Acts 2:16–17; Gal 4:4; 1 Cor 10:11; 2 Cor 6:2; 1 Tim 4:1; 2 Tim 3:1; 1 Pet 1:20; 2 Pet 3:3; Heb 1:2; 9:26; Jas 5:3; 1 John 2:18; Jude 18.

VISIONS OF VICTORY

John not only repeats visions of the final judgment, the last battle, the fall of Babylon, and the three-and-a-half years; he also uses repetition for visions of victory and rest. Visions of believers in rest or victory appear throughout the book: 6:9–11; 7:9–17; 11:15–18; 14:1–5, 13; 15:2–4; 19:1–9; 20:4–6; and 21:1–22:5. These visions connect to the promises made to the ones who overcome at the end of each of the proclamations to the seven churches in chapters 2 and 3. There are too many parallels between these various visions of victory for us to list them here. It is not always clear whether they are describing God's victorious people in the intermediate state (the time between death and final resurrection) or in final resurrection life in God's new creation. In some of the visions (particularly 7:9–17), the intermediate state and final state seem to be blended together as John moves seamlessly from describing one to describing the other. Here is just a brief sample of some of these visions.

Rev 7:16–17	Rev 14:13	Rev 15:2
They shall hunger no more, neither thirst anymore; the sun shall not strike them, nor any scorching heat. For the Lamb in the midst of the throne will be their shepherd, and he will guide them to springs of living water, and God will wipe away every tear from their eyes.	And I heard a voice from heaven saying, "Write this: Blessed are the dead who die in the Lord from now on." "Blessed indeed," says the Spirit, "that they may rest from their labors, for their deeds follow them!"	And I saw what appeared to be a sea of glass mingled with fire—and also those who had conquered the beast and its image and the number of its name, standing beside the sea of glass with harps of God in their hands.

Rev 20:4	Rev 21:3–4
Also I saw the souls of those who had been beheaded for the testimony of Jesus and for the word of God, and those who had not worshiped the beast or its image and had not received its mark on their foreheads or their hands. They came to life and reigned with Christ for a thousand years.	Behold, the dwelling place of God is with man. He will dwell with them, and they will be his people, and God himself will be with them as their God. He will wipe away every tear from their eyes, and death shall be no more, neither shall there be mourning, nor crying, nor pain anymore, for the former things have passed away.

There is no need to try to fit these visions of victory into a chronological timeline of end-time events. They are describing either disembodied believers between death and final resurrection (the intermediate state) or eternal resurrection life in God's new creation. Clearly, John alternates his visions of judgment with visions of salvation. These visions of salvation do not describe a series of different time periods and events but rather assure us that even if we must suffer now through persecution, rejection, poverty, sickness, and difficulties, we can have confidence that we will experience vindication and rest immediately after death and eternal resurrection life in God's new creation.

OLD TESTAMENT EXAMPLES OF VISIONARY REPETITION

Although we could discuss many more examples of repetition in Revelation's visions, the ones above demonstrate the point. Before moving on, however, we should note that John is not alone in his use of visionary repetition. This practice is common among the Old Testament prophets, and John is completely in line with their use of visionary repetition.

Take Daniel as an example. Five of Daniel's visions evidence repetition of the same time period and the same events from different perspectives and with different degrees of detail. Daniel 2 describes a statue made of four different types of metal. The different metals symbolize a succession of four different kingdoms, which would culminate with the coming of the kingdom of God. The vision of Daniel 7 describes the same four kingdoms culminating in the kingdom of God, but it pictures them as ferocious beasts. Daniel is describing the same thing with different details and from a different perspective. In chapter 8, he focuses in more detail on two of the kingdoms and describes their conflict as that between a ram and a goat. Chapter 9 describes the time period using a numerical system (seventy weeks), but it is the same period that culminates in the coming kingdom of God. Finally, the vision in chapter 11 of the kings from the north and the south focuses on a part of that time period and likewise brings its readers to the end. Daniel's entire book is structured like Revelation. The visions more or less keep covering the same time period, with a similar end point but with different details and from different perspectives.

Isaiah and Ezekiel also contain many clear examples of repetition in their prophecies, although there is no need to go into specific details here. The main point is that to read John's visions as repeatedly covering the same time period and bringing hearers to the same end point is to read him as we read the other main biblical prophets. Based on the Hebrew prophets, John's use of visionary repetition should be entirely expected.

ARGUMENTS AGAINST REPETITION

The main argument against repetition is that John's visions seem to intensify as the book unfolds. The fourth seal affects 25% of the people on the earth, the first four trumpets affect 33% of the physical universe (trees, sea, springs, cosmic lights), the fifth trumpet seems to affect 100% of unbelievers, the sixth trumpet kills 33% of mankind, and the seven bowls seem to be universal and affect

100% of unbelievers, the sea, and springs. So, in general, there is a progression in intensity as the visions of judgment develop throughout the narrative. This is not consistent, however, and we already noted how the sixth and seventh seals are universal, affecting everyone and everything.

Instead of requiring sequential chronological progression in the visions, the intensification simply indicates that things will get worse as we move closer to the end. When we claim that the visions in Revelation largely repeat themselves and each vision moves the hearer from their present time until the final judgment, we are not claiming that the visions are exact in every way. They are quite diverse, but they all describe the same story of judgment being poured out throughout time, culminating in the final judgment. Some interpreters describe this forward progression blended with repetition as a spiral.

WHY REPETITION?

Remembering our first principle from chapter 1 (focus on the original purpose of the visions), we can explore how the intensified repetition impacts us as readers. How does it motivate us to action, stir us to repentance, and persuade us to persevere in faithfulness to the end? In this case, the repeated but intensified descriptions of judgment keep us on the edge of our seats waiting and longing for the end to finally come, waiting to finally read the last visions of eternal life in God's new creation in Revelation 21–22. The intensification stirs emotions of fear, and possibly even terror, among those who know they are living in rebellion against God. Similarly, those who are faithfully persevering through suffering draw comfort and hope from the repeated visions of victory and rest. The repetition, which keeps delaying the end, also helps us to understand the current delay in Christ's return. We want him to return just as we want to reach the final visions of the book, but there is a delay, during which we suffer but must bear faithful witness.

CONCLUSION: RECOGNIZE REPETITION

If you seek to read John's visions in a chronologically sequential way, you will forever remain confused and be forced to make up explanations to try to make things fit. You will also have a long and complicated chart of end-time events. It is easier to herd cats together for a family portrait with young children than to provide a convincing chronologically sequential explanation of the visions.

In contrast, the simple principle discussed in this chapter—recognize repetition—will help things fall into place. This principle does not tell you in advance whether there are two final battles or just one, but it alerts you to the fact that the visions in Revelation regularly cover the same basic sequence of events with additional details from various perspectives. This is in line with the practice of the prophets in the Old Testament and is what we should expect when approaching John's visionary and prophetic messages in Revelation.

Revelation is primarily composed of a series of visions that describe the time between Jesus's first and second comings as judgment, conflict (battle/warfare), and persecution. The visions make it clear that this period will culminate with Jesus's return and both the final judgment of all those who oppose God and his people and vindication, rest, and final salvation for all who overcome. Recognize repetition when you see it.

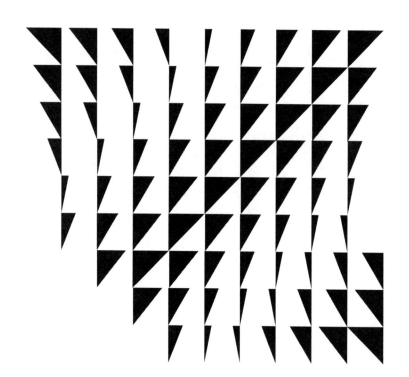

CHAPTER 4

Symbolism: More Than Meets the Eye

PRINCIPLE #4
RECOGNIZE SYMBOLISM.

Figurative language is so common that we hardly recognize it in normal conversations. Symbolic and figurative language is just as common in the Bible, particularly in psalms, poetry, wisdom literature, and apocalyptic passages.

It has often been taught that we should seek to interpret the visions in Revelation as literally as possible. This approach is built on the argument that we should interpret all of Scripture literally unless there are significant, compelling, and explicit reasons to look for a figurative meaning. This sounds like common sense and resonates with those of us who value Scripture and want to interpret it accurately, but when applied to Revelation, it leads to literalistic misreadings. The problem is that the principle of literal interpretation, as generally understood, puts the cart before the horse. The goal is not to interpret literally but to understand, as much as we possibly can, the author's intended meaning. Now if the author intended to write in a literal way, which is normally the case in historical narratives and biography, then a

49

literal interpretation is the best way to properly understand the intended meaning. Conversely, however, if the author intended to write using symbolism, then a literal interpretation will lead to an interpretive train wreck. Literal interpretation of a symbolic vision will lead to misinterpretation just as quickly as a symbolic interpretation of literal communication. There is no one-size-fits-all approach to interpreting different literary genres. The goal is to determine how the author intended to communicate and interpret accordingly.

SYMBOLIC VISIONS

There are three compelling reasons for considering John's visions to be heavily symbolic.

First, and most obviously, Revelation fits within the genre of apocalyptic literature. This genre is saturated with symbolic and figurative language. Revelation is not the only book in antiquity within the apocalyptic genre. Other books and parts of books include Daniel; Isaiah 24–27, 56–66; Ezekiel 38–39; Joel 3–4; Zechariah 9–14; 1 Enoch; 2 Enoch; 3 Enoch; 4 Ezra; 2 Baruch; the Testament of Moses; and many of the Dead Sea Scrolls. These latter books may sound unfamiliar to you, but they are Jewish apocalyptic writings that help shape our understanding of the apocalyptic genre. There is no need for an extensive discussion of genre at this point beyond the simple observation that Revelation shares various features with these other books. These shared features include the extensive use of symbolic visions.

We discussed Daniel in chapter 3 with regard to visionary repetition, but it is also worth mentioning him here. Daniel 2 describes four kingdoms (probably Babylon, Persia, Greece, and Rome) as different metals in a unified statue, while the coming of Jesus and the establishment of his kingdom are symbolically described as a "stone … cut from a mountain by no human hand" that smashes the fourth kingdom (Dan 2:45). The stone then grows into a huge mountain. Daniel 7 describes the same nations as four grotesque and distorted beasts. Daniel 8 describes the conflict between two of these kingdoms, symbolically described as a ram and a goat (Medo-Persia and Greece). Symbolic visions are used throughout Daniel to communicate his message of hope for God's future salvation. When reading Daniel, our default assumption is that the visions are communicating their meaning through symbolic descriptions of things and events. The same is true for Revelation. If it looks like a fish, smells like a fish, and feels like a fish, we should not assume it is a dog and try to teach it to play catch and roll over. Similarly, we need to recognize that Revelation looks, smells, and feels similar to the visions in Daniel and other examples of apocalyptic literature and stop trying to make it act like a straightforward, literal historical narrative of future events.

Second, in Revelation 1:1, John uses the Greek word *sēmainō* (report, communicate by signs, suggest, signify) to describe the visions he received:[1] "The revelation of Jesus Christ, which God gave him to show to his servants the things that must soon take place. He *made it known* [*sēmainō*] by sending his angel to his servant John." *Sēmainō* can simply mean "report," "show," "communicate," or "make known," depending on the context, but it often indicates that there is a deeper meaning to some symbolic action or saying. It is related to the noun for "sign" (*sēmeion*). The Delphic Oracle was the most famous location in the ancient world to which people traveled to get divine advice. The oracle would often answer someone's question, but in an ambiguous or confusing way. Stories abound in ancient literature of people who misinterpreted the oracle's message and ended up in disaster. *Sēmainō* is used for the need to interpret the real or deeper meaning of the oracle's message (Heraclitus, Fragment 93). Philo of Alexandria likewise uses *sēmainō* to describe the hidden, deeper meaning or significance

---

1. For a fuller discussion of *sēmainō* and arguments in favor of a symbolic interpretation of Revelation, see G. K. Beale, *The Book of Revelation*, NIGTC (Grand Rapids: Eerdmans, 1999), 50–55.

of the Old Testament or of a particular word. Most relevant for our purpose, John himself uses it in contexts in which Jesus "signifies" his manner of death and Peter's in symbolic or veiled language that requires deeper interpretation (John 12:33; 18:32; 21:19). All of this suggests that John uses *sēmainō* in Revelation 1:1 as an indication of the symbolic nature of the visions to follow—they will need to be interpreted to arrive at the deeper intended meaning.

Third, each of the seven proclamations to the churches in Revelation 2–3 ends with a similar phrase: "He who has an ear, let him hear what the Spirit says to the churches." This phrase deliberately echoes Jesus's use of the same expression throughout the Gospels as a formulaic command to understand the message of his symbolic parables. Jesus particularly used it to indicate that the elect will be able to understand, while unbelievers will fail to understand and will reject the message (Matt 13:9–17; Mark 4:9, 23; Luke 8:8). The expression occurs again in the middle of Revelation during the vision of the two beasts: "If anyone has an ear, let him hear: If anyone is to be taken captive, to captivity he goes; if anyone is to be slain with the sword, with the sword must he be slain. Here is a call for the endurance and faith of the saints" (13:9–10). John's visions require ears to hear. There is a deeper meaning that will be veiled to outsiders but understandable to those with ears to hear what the Spirit is speaking.

These three considerations make it virtually certain that John's visions were meant to be heavily symbolic, and attempts to interpret them literalistically will go against the author's intended meaning.

SYMBOLIC LANGUAGE WITH EXPLICIT INTERPRETATION

Sometimes John tells us what the symbols mean. We might wish that he did this more often, but we can be thankful for every bit of help. In Revelation 1:20, he informs us of the meaning of some of the elements in the previous vision. The stars represent angels, and the seven lampstands represent the seven churches. Knowing that the lampstand symbol is used for churches also helps us understand the identity of the two witnesses in chapter 11 when they are described as "two lampstands" (11:4). The connection of stars to angels does not mean that every mention of stars in Revelation should be interpreted as angels, but it does indicate that this possibility should be kept in mind. The language in 6:13 probably does not have angels in mind when it speaks about the stars falling because it is one item among others in a more comprehensive description of cosmic upheaval. On the other hand, it is likely that the dragon sweeping one third of the stars to earth in 12:4 points toward demons since later in the vision, it is mentioned that he was thrown to earth with his angels (12:9). The fallen star of 8:10 and 9:1 should also be understood to refer to a spiritual being.

John helpfully tells us that the seven torches of fire before God's throne are the seven spirits of God (4:5), and the Lamb's seven eyes are also the seven spirits of God (5:6). Symbolic apocalyptic visions defy all attempts at perfect systematization. The seven spirits of God are symbolically described two different ways in two consecutive chapters. Instead of being a contradiction, each symbolic description helps us understand more about God's Spirit. Throughout Revelation, communication of symbolic meaning is more important than logical consistency.

In 5:8, John tells us that the bowls of incense are the prayers of the saints, and in 19:8, we read that the fine linen of the Lamb's bride is the righteous deeds of the saints. These are just some examples in which John provides explicit interpretation of the symbols in his visions. More often than not, however, he leaves it up to the spiritual discernment of the hearer to properly interpret his meaning: "He who has an ear, let him hear what the Spirit says to the churches" (2:7, 11, 17, 29; 3:6, 13, 22).

GUIDELINES

The symbolic nature of the book does not mean that the symbols are completely open to any interpretation. This is probably the biggest fear motivating those who argue for a literal interpretation: if we acknowledge that the visions should be interpreted symbolically, we will open a Pandora's box for people to make all sorts of crazy claims. Perhaps crazy is in the eye of the beholder, since a literal interpretation of many of John's visions leads to some bizarre and even theologically problematic conclusions.

Symbols cannot mean anything we want them to mean. They are not Play-Doh that can be rolled into a snake one minute and then transformed into a pancake the next, or a Rorschach test in which the inkblot can be anything the viewer claims it is. The historical, literary, and theological context helps us understand what the symbols likely meant to the first hearers and still mean for us today. Symbols have a real referent and point to true realities.

Several guidelines can help us properly interpret John's symbolism. Let's start with the principles for interpreting Revelation discussed above. Principle 3, about John's use of visionary repetition, indicates that if several visions can be identified as being roughly parallel to each other, then they can be used to help interpret each other. John's use of visionary repetition can help us understand what is going on in particularly difficult visions. Take, for example, God's seal mentioned in Revelation 7:2–8 and 9:4. The broader theological context of the New Testament might lead us to connect this seal with the Holy Spirit since this is what Paul normally has in mind when he talks about God's seal (2 Cor 1:22; Eph 1:13; 4:30). This interpretation might make sense of the vision, but John himself does not make this connection in Revelation and instead points us to a different aspect of God's seal. Later references to this same group of people, the 144,000, suggest that the seal is Jesus's and God's name written on their foreheads (Rev 14:1). Revelation 22:4 indicates that all God's people in his future new creation have his name on their foreheads. So for John, God's seal is his name, which signifies ownership and protection. This also suggests that the 144,000 may be a symbolic number for all of God's people—all those who have his name on their forehead and will experience resurrection life in God's new creation (more on the 144,000 later).

Principle 2, regarding the importance of the historical context, also plays an essential role here. Do other ancient authors use or discuss the same symbolic images? For example, the connection of fallen stars to fallen angels was widespread in other apocalyptic literature of the time and helps confirm our interpretation of the stars of Revelation 12:4 as fallen angels.

Principle 5 (discussed in the next chapter) also draws our attention to the use of the Old Testament in Revelation. John depended heavily on the Old Testament, and we can often find clues to proper interpretation of his symbolic visions by considering the use of similar images, words, and scenarios in the Old Testament. The Old Testament is significant in both big and small ways. A big example is how John's descriptions of the seven trumpets and bowls contain plagues, which are similar to the ten plagues directed against Egypt in Exodus. A small example is the way that the two witnesses are described as consuming their enemies with fire from their mouths (11:5). Some popular interpreters take this literally and visualize two fire-breathing individuals. I remember watching a movie about the end times that took this interpretive approach. Two human flame-throwers opened their mouths and breathed fire on the surrounding guards. In contrast, we should first note that most things coming out of people's mouths in Revelation are symbolic (for example, the swords in 1:16; 2:12, 16; 19:15, 21 and the frogs in 16:13–14). Then, we should consider that in the broader historical context, a contemporary Jewish apocalyptic book describes the Messiah as destroying Israel's enemies by fire proceeding from his mouth, which is interpreted as the law (4 Ezra 13:25–39). Finally, and most importantly, Jeremiah 5:14 notes, "Because you have spoken this word, behold, I am making my words in your mouth a fire ... and the fire shall consume them." Jeremiah's message from God is described as a fire that consumes his hearers who reject his message. The message of the two witnesses in Revelation 11:5 should be understood similarly; there is no need to suggest apocalyptic human flame-throwers.

Remember that a legitimate symbolic interpretation involves identifying the symbolic meaning intended by the author. There is no need for fanciful allegory or creative and imaginative speculation unless there are good reasons to suspect that such was John's intent. As the old saying goes, context is king. We need to interpret in light of the literary context (the immediate passage, the whole book of Revelation, the entire Bible), the historical context (including the broader Jewish and Greco-Roman culture), and the theological context.

WHY SYMBOLS?

The apocalyptic genre strikes many readers today as quite strange. We immediately want to decode the visions and provide an explanation for every symbolic detail. We should resist this urge. Some of the details do not have specific meanings but serve as special effects to add vividness to the scene. Many of the symbolic details seek to impact our emotions more than our minds. Try reading Revelation 9 and then a commentary on Revelation 9. The vision by itself is terrifying and incredibly emotional. The commentary on the vision, however, is far less likely to impact you emotionally. The commentary will explain some of the details and provide understanding for your mind, but it is not likely to move you. Emotions are not intrinsically bad and should not be carelessly suppressed. They were created by God and are an essential part of what it means to be human. Symbolism is aimed at both the head and the heart.

CONCLUSION

To read the visions symbolically, in line with the rest of the poetic and apocalyptic imagery in the Bible, is to read the text as it was intended to be interpreted; it is not twisting the text. A literal reading of a symbolic text will distort the intended meaning. In light of the evidence discussed above, the traditional interpretive maxim should be turned upside down. Instead of seeking the literal meaning, unless there are compelling reasons otherwise, we should assume a symbolic meaning for the visions in Revelation unless there are compelling reasons to read them literally. Symbolic and not literal interpretation should be the default approach for Revelation.

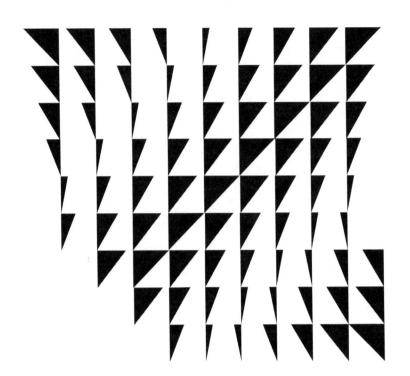

CHAPTER 5

Christian Scripture: The Whole
Is More Than Its Parts

PRINCIPLE #5
READ REVELATION AS CHRISTIAN SCRIPTURE.

For some readers, this final principle may seem like nothing more than stating the obvious. Of course, Revelation is part of the Bible; how could anyone miss this point? It is valuable, however, to consider two important implications of this principle. First, because it is Christian Scripture, it has a theological contribution to make. That is, we should be alert as we read Revelation to how it can shape our thoughts about God, Jesus, the Holy Spirit, sin, salvation, the church, the world, and the future. Second, as mentioned in the previous chapter, the Old Testament is essential for understanding John's visions because there are so many intentional connections. It is evident that John thought his visions were a continuation of the Old Testament. There are particularly strong connections to the books of Ezekiel, Daniel, Isaiah, Psalms, Exodus, and Zechariah. Allusions to the Old Testament saturate Revelation and are essential to proper interpretation.

The visions within Revelation are rightly understood only when viewed in light of the whole of Scripture. They find their place, their purpose, and their meaning as the continuation and fulfillment of the great story of Scripture that begins with Genesis.

SEEING THE BIG PICTURE

The very first book in the Bible, Genesis, describes how God created the world and human beings to serve as his representatives, to rule on his behalf in his creation. Being deceived by the serpent, the first humans rebelled against God's authority and commands. God's plan for humanity seemed to fail at that point. Because of the entrance of sin and death, human beings were not able to serve effectively as God's representative rulers in his creation. In God's judgment of the serpent, he declares, "I will put enmity between you and the woman, and between your offspring and her offspring; he shall bruise your head, and you shall bruise his heel" (Gen 3:15). This statement is a bit enigmatic but seems to suggest ongoing conflict between the seed of the woman (human beings) and the serpent, a conflict in which humans would one day gain the upper hand. The word for "seed" is famously ambiguous and, because it is a collective term, could point to an individual seed, a single individual, or a multitude of descendants. Genesis, by itself, does not narrate the solution to this catastrophe or bring closure.

Several visions in Revelation directly build upon Genesis 1–3 and describe God's solution and the final fulfillment of his plans. First, the vision in Revelation 12 has as its main characters a woman, a son, the ancient serpent, and other descendants of the woman (described in Greek as "the rest of her seed" in 12:17). This cast of characters is hardly coincidental, and when read in light of Genesis 3:15, the vision makes sense. Revelation 12 narrates how the singular seed, Jesus, was enthroned in heaven and the devil was defeated. The conflict, however, would continue on earth, with the serpent trying to destroy the rest of God's people.

Second, the vision in Revelation 21–22:5 shows how human beings will one day have access to the tree of life, will live in direct relationship with God, and will fulfill the purpose for which God first created humanity, to reign on the earth. Genesis by itself does not show how God will bring a solution to the problems of sin and death, and Revelation by itself assumes readers have some understanding of the problem to which it describes the solution. The first and last chapters of the Bible show a remarkable narrative and theological unity. They move from creation to new creation and from a vision of God walking among humanity in the garden to God dwelling with humanity in his new creation. They move from God's curse on humanity because of rebellion to the removal of the curse and God's blessing on restored humanity. John intended his visions to be read together with the Old Testament as part of one great story, the story of God, his world, and his people. Revelation invites us to find ourselves in this story. We are characters in the great conflict. We will experience suffering, but we are promised an incredible future.

CHRISTIAN THEOLOGY: JESUS

One example should illustrate Revelation's contribution to Christian theology: Revelation helps us better understand the relationship between Jesus and God. They are never collapsed into each other, and they maintain their distinct identities; they are two persons. They are also, however, closely linked together in significant ways; they are so close, in fact, that Christians speak of one God—we do not worship two Gods. The New Testament never uses the word "Trinity," but it does provide the foundation for later Christian theological reflection on what it means for there to be one God but three persons.

Jesus receives worship along with God in a way that other angels and human beings do not (Rev 5:13); Jesus is not just another angel. Jesus is also described as sharing God's throne (3:21; 22:1);

nobody else has that right or privilege. The day of the Lord from the Old Testament is transformed in Revelation into the day of the Lord and the Lamb (6:17). The Old Testament prophets regularly spoke for God with the phrase, "Thus says the Lord," but in Revelation, Jesus speaks in that way to God's people (2:1, 8, 12, 18; 3:1, 7, 14). God's people are sealed with the name of both God and the Lamb (14:1). God and the Lamb function together as the replacement for the temple in the New Jerusalem (21:22), and both fill it with light (21:23). In 1:8, God describes himself as the "Alpha and the Omega," and Jesus also describes himself as "the Alpha and the Omega, the first and the last, the beginning and the end" (22:13).

John doesn't explicitly claim that God and Jesus are both united and distinct, but it is easy to see how later Christians drew those conclusions from the way John describes their relationship. They go together and are connected in a way unparalleled in the universe. The Holy Spirit is also quite active in Revelation and is described as the seven spirits before God's throne (1:4; 4:5) who are also intimately connected with Jesus as the Lamb's seven eyes (5:6). Everything Jesus says to the churches in Revelation 2–3 is also described as what the Spirit is saying to the churches (2:7, 11, 17, 29; 3:6, 13, 22). John sends greetings to the churches from God, Jesus, and the Spirit (1:4–5). All of this suggests a close and intimate relationship among the Father, the Son, and the Spirit. They can be understood as one (monotheism) without losing their individual identities. John doesn't use the word "Trinity," but he provides the conceptual material needed to develop that later theological conclusion.

THE PROMISE TO ABRAHAM

Another important example of the importance of reading Revelation as Christian Scripture comes when we consider God's promise to Abraham that he would give him innumerable descendants (Gen 13:16; 15:5; 32:12; Hos 1:10). Revelation 7:9 alludes to this promise when John sees "a great multitude *that no one could number*, from every nation, from all tribes and peoples and languages, standing before the throne and before the Lamb, clothed in white robes, with palm branches in their hands." This vision of victory for God's people builds on God's promise to Abraham but universalizes it to include those from every nation, tribe, people, and language, in a manner that suggests fulfillment. God's goal for humanity is not limited to ethnic Israelites but includes people from every ethnicity, nation, and language! This is not anti-Semitic and does not exclude Jews because John himself was Jewish, and he clearly included Jewish believers in this group. For John, God was not unfaithful to his promise to Abraham about his physical descendants but fulfilled it in a way that went far beyond the original promise.

This conclusion fits well with New Testament theology as a whole; we see Paul make a similar argument in Romans 4. There, Paul argues that Abraham was the father of all who believe, whether they were ethnically Jewish or not (Rom 4:11–12, 16–17; compare Gal 3:29). That is why non-Jewish Christians can also look to Abraham as their father in the faith.

This expansion of the promise is something like if I promised my son that for his birthday I would give ice cream to everyone in our family. When the day finally came, I fulfilled my promise to give ice cream to everyone in the family, but I also turned it into a block party and gave ice cream to everyone living on our street, even people my son did not know very well or at all. I did not fail in my promise, but I expanded the promise to include non-family members. The expansion of the promise does not undermine the original promise.

For John, Christian believers (both Jew and non-Jew) bring fulfillment to God's promises to Abraham about his innumerable descendants. Instead of ethnicity or physical descent, John makes allegiance to Jesus the key determining characteristic of God's people. This is made clear when we notice how John alludes to Exodus 19:3–6. This passage records the first words spoken by

God to the people after they had escaped Egypt and arrived at Mt. Sinai. It communicates God's goal in rescuing the people of Israel.

> Thus you shall say to the house of Jacob, and tell the people of Israel: "You yourselves have seen what I did to the Egyptians, and how I bore you on eagles' wings and brought you to myself. Now therefore, if you will indeed obey my voice and keep my covenant, you shall be my treasured possession among all peoples, for all the earth is mine; and you shall be to me a *kingdom of priests* and a holy nation." (Exod 19:3–6)

God rescued the Israelites in order to make them into a kingdom of priests and a holy nation, his treasured possession. John alludes to Exodus 19:6 with a strong sense of fulfillment in two key places (see also Rev 20:6):

> To him who loves us and has freed us from our sins by his blood and *made us a kingdom, priests* to his God and Father. (Rev 1:5–6)

> Worthy are you to take the scroll and to open its seals, for you were slain, and by your blood you ransomed people for God from every tribe and language and people and nation, and *you have made them a kingdom and priests* to our God. (Rev 5:9–10)

For John, Christ's work of salvation (freeing his people from sins and ransoming them by his blood) succeeded in creating a kingdom of priests to serve God and reign on the earth. John presents this kingdom of priests as the fulfillment of what God originally intended for the Hebrew people when he rescued them from Egypt many years before. The fulfillment of God's plan as expressed in Exodus 19:6 comes not through a renewed ethnic or national Israel but through the purchase of people from every tribe, tongue, people, and nation (Rev 5:9). The activity of this people (both Jew and gentile) as a kingdom of priests had already begun with Jesus's death and resurrection. We as Jewish and non-Jewish Christians currently constitute God's kingdom and function as priests, mediators of God's presence to the world.

As we work through Revelation in Part 2, we will see many examples of how John freely applies Old Testament promises, made to ethnic Israel, to the church in the first century, which was made up of both Jews and gentiles. It did not take long in church history for non-Jewish Christians to begin arguing that the church had replaced Israel. This claim, known as supersessionism, is not how the first-century Christians thought. Throughout the New Testament, the "church" is described in Jewish terms, and almost all the first Christians were Jewish. As the first century progressed, gentiles were added to the Jewish faith in Jesus as the Messiah. Gentiles were added to or included within Israel through faith, conversion, and baptism. This took place through the ministries of Peter with Cornelius, Philip with the Samaritans, and Paul and his associates throughout the Greco-Roman world. These gentile Christians were viewed never as replacing ethnic Jews but as being included in Israel's restoration through the Messiah in fulfillment of God's Old Testament promises about Israel's future. The church in the New Testament is the fulfillment of God's promises to Israel, but it is not a gentile or non-Jewish fulfillment. The Christian church is a Jewish fulfillment of God's promises to Israel, in which non-Jews are included. This perspective opposes both those who argue that the church replaced Israel and those who argue that the church and Israel are completely distinct. Both of these approaches misunderstand the Jewish-focused and Israel-centered nature of the church in the New Testament.

This discussion of the fulfillment of God's promises to Abraham and the fulfillment of his purposes in rescuing the tribes of Israel from Egypt demonstrates the strong connections between Revelation and the Old Testament. John's visions explicitly build on the Old Testament and find their meaning in relationship to the promises in the Old Testament. Revelation can only be rightly understood when it is read as Christian Scripture.

CONCLUSION

Reading Revelation in isolation from the rest of the Bible is somewhat like watching a 3D movie without the 3D glasses. You will be able to follow the general plot because of the dialogue, but everything will be blurry. Important details will be impossible to see, and you will probably end up with a headache. The viewing experience will be miserable and deeply unsatisfying; it will certainly not be what the filmmaker intended it to be.

There is a danger, of course, of using other books in the Bible to force interpretations on Revelation that distort the main points of the visions. This happens when someone takes a phrase from Daniel, combines it with a verse from the Olivet Discourse in Matthew, mixes it with a sentence from Paul in 1 or 2 Thessalonians, and pronounces the meaning of a vision in Revelation. The end result of this kind of approach is an interpretation that doesn't actually fit any of the original contexts. You should be suspicious of interpretations that depend on taking phrases from multiple books to create a new scenario or new vision not contained in any of the original passages.

Reading Revelation as Christian Scripture requires that we remain alert to the theological implications of John's visions and how they build on and are informed by the Old Testament and broader New Testament teaching. As you approach each vision, it is important to ask: What does this vision teach me about God, Jesus, sin, salvation, and God's people? Also, how does this fit with what I know to be true about these topics from other Old Testament and New Testament books?

THE VISIONS

Seeing Reality

Having considered five foundational interpretive principles in Part 1, we are now ready to look more closely at how the visions of Revelation pull back the curtain and enable readers to see reality from God's perspective. In Part 2, we will work through the book step by step. Each chapter will consider a section of Revelation or a sequence of visions. The chapters will begin with summary statements called "Seeing the Big Picture"; these statements will seek to succinctly summarize the main points of the visions under consideration. The chapters will then provide an overview of the visions. We will not be able to look at every detail, every symbol, or every verse, but the chapters in Part 2 will help you gain a clear understanding of the meaning and main points of each vision based on the five principles discussed in Part 1. At the end of Part 2, you should be able to understand Revelation and even explain it to others! Most importantly, you will hopefully feel the motivational force of the book and hear God's message to you through it. It is not enough to simply know more if we remain unchanged by what we know. Knowledge is essential, but it is not enough. We must overcome! May God enable us to respond rightly to the knowledge we have

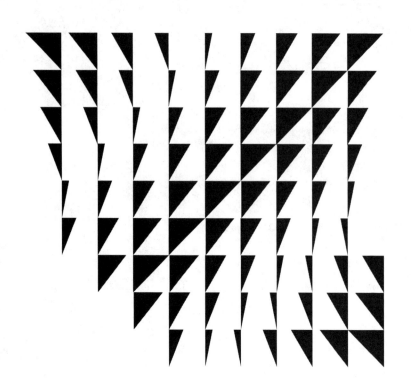

CHAPTER 6

Establishing Authority

Why should I listen? Why should I obey? Why should I do what someone tells me to do? Our current culture has an authority problem. We have convinced ourselves that we are in charge of our fate. We determine our destiny. We think we should have unlimited freedom to do whatever we want to do. We are suspicious of anyone who would dare to tell us what to do or how we ought to live.

It is true, of course, that authority can be abused. Evil people oppress and abuse others, and when evil people gain authority, those under their power get hurt. It is essential for authority to be legitimate and for people in authority to be good. Many people, however, assume that all authority is oppressive; they lack a category for good and legitimate authority. They naively think that it is possible to live life free from authority, free from constraints, free from rules, free from obsolete and ancient ideas about right and wrong or good and evil.

Revelation presents a very different perspective on the world. God is the ultimate legitimate authority. This authority is grounded in the fact that he created everything that exists (Rev 4:11; 10:6; 14:7). Human beings are accountable to God for how we live our lives. Fortunately, God is also good, just, and kind. His judgment is not random, mean, indiscriminate, or excessive; judgment functions to destroy the ones destroying the earth (Rev 11:18). God's judgment of evil functions like a surgeon removing a cancerous tumor. The cancer (evil) is destroying and corrupting the entire body, and the body cannot be whole again until the cancer is removed. God's world is pictured as broken by evil, and the judgment and removal of evil is necessary for the world to be whole again.

Seeing the Big Picture

- Revelation 1 introduces us to the key characters: God, Jesus, the Spirit, and John.

- God's authority stands behind the message and visions of Revelation. We can trust John's message in Revelation because it comes from Jesus to God's people.

Revelation also places strong demands on you, its reader. It calls you to overcome and gain the victory over evil in life (see the portrait of an overcomer in chapter 1 above). This victory will not come for free; there is an incredible cost involved. John's visions tell us that we will suffer in this life. We will be actively opposed, persecuted, and possibly even killed by God's adversaries (Rev 13). We must trust God that it is worth it, that the battle against evil and sin will be worth it in the end. This is a trust in God's faithfulness and authority. It is a trust that God has the rightful authority to command us to live a certain way, even when that command puts constraints on our autonomy, our desire to do whatever we feel like in the moment. God has the authority to command us to live in a way that will involve sacrifice and hardship.

This not only requires a trust in God's rightful authority; it also requires trust in God's spokesperson. Who has the authority to speak for God, to communicate God's will to human beings? Can that person be trusted? What happens when multiple people claim to speak for God but tell us contradictory things? This is the situation in which John's first hearers found themselves and in which we find ourselves today. John was not the only prophetic leader in

these churches, and his was not the only option. As we will see in
the next chapter, on Revelation 2–3, other Christian leaders were
active in the churches, and they were proclaiming a very different
message from John's.

As we saw in chapter 1, Revelation calls us to overcome through
persevering in obedience to God's commands, witnessing to God's
victory through his Messiah Jesus, and worshiping God for his
power, love, and salvation. The refusal to worship the Roman
emperor or the deities of local trade guilds would lead to the loss
of work opportunities, to suspicion, and to direct persecution.
Other Christian leaders were not so rigorous or demanding. They
promoted a form of Christianity that fit in much better with the
broader culture. Their version of Christianity was less distinct,
and it wouldn't be seen as strange or a threat to those with power
and influence. If we do not seek to bear witness to Jesus as Lord,
we will not draw attention to ourselves, we will not make enemies,
and we will fit in. If we are willing to bow down to the gods of our
culture alongside our worship of Jesus, we will not face opposition or persecution.

The Christians in the seven churches addressed in Revelation
were being confronted with a choice between two versions of
Christianity. One version would lead to much more success in this
life. They could believe in Jesus but keep it to themselves. They
could become wealthy and have influence in society by not making
waves, by fitting in. The other version, promoted by John, required
a way of life that would lead to opposition and rejection by their
neighbors, friends, and colleagues. It would bear witness to Jesus
as the only hope and would call on their neighbors to repent and
change their way of life in light of God's judgment of sin. It would
refuse to simply fit in with the broader culture. It would likely lead
to increasing poverty.

The Christians who first read Revelation were confronted with
a choice, the same choice that confronts you today. John knew that
this was not an easy choice to make. He knew that some hearers

would not trust him and would prefer to follow the Christian leaders who taught an easy version of Christianity to avoid persecution and achieve financial stability and social acceptance.

Revelation 1 sets the stage for the whole book by establishing authority. Do God and Jesus have the rightful authority to make claims on our lives, and does John have the authority to speak on God's behalf and communicate God's message to his people? This may seem obvious to us today because Revelation is included in the Bible, but when John first wrote the book, it was not part of the Bible, and the first Christian hearers had to evaluate John's claims. Should John be trusted as communicating God's authoritative message to his people?

THE CHAIN OF AUTHORITY

Revelation 1:1–2 establishes a chain of communication and authority. God provides the revelation about Jesus Christ to his people by sending his angel to John.

> The revelation of Jesus Christ, which God gave him to show to his servants the things that must soon take place. He made it known by sending his angel to his servant John, who bore witness to the word of God and to the testimony of Jesus Christ, even to all that he saw.

This introduction makes several claims: (1) God is the ultimate source of the message of Revelation; (2) angels serve to communicate this message; and (3) John is simply bearing witness to what he saw, not inventing the message. The original hearers or modern readers could, of course, dispute John's claims and argue that he was just making it all up to gain power and influence for himself in the churches. This suspicion is not automatically irreverent or wrong, since we are taught throughout the Bible that God's people must test and evaluate prophecy. How should Revelation be evaluated? I suggest that principle 5, discussed in the prior chapter, is key: is there theological and narrative continuity between

Revelation and the rest of Scripture, or does John go beyond prior authoritative revelation from God? Revelation demonstrates strong continuity throughout; that is, John is not inventing things or going beyond what was taught in the Old Testament or by Jesus and Paul but rather is calling God's people to radical faithfulness to the truth. This is exactly what the Old Testament prophets did. John's message in Revelation fits well within Christian Scripture.

John does not directly identify himself as the apostle John or the author of the Gospel of John, although the earliest Christians made this connection. John instead presents himself as a Christian prophet in line with the Old Testament prophets by describing Revelation as a prophecy (1:3; 10:11; 22:7, 9, 10, 18, 19). There are good reasons to think that the same John wrote the Gospel, the three letters, and Revelation, but since John does not explicitly make this claim, it is not necessary for properly understanding Revelation.

John describes himself in 1:9 as "your brother and partner in the tribulation and the kingdom and the patient endurance that are in Jesus." This statement establishes camaraderie between John and his hearers. He was their brother, not physically, but spiritually, in God's multiethnic family. He was also their partner in three things: tribulation, the kingdom, and endurance. The fact that he was also suffering with them helps build our confidence in him. John was not like a modern-day prosperity preacher, with private jets, thousand-dollar outfits, and million-dollar homes. He was in the trenches with his fellow Christians. He experienced hardship and poverty just as they did. Suffering served to validate his message. His faithful witness to Jesus led to suffering, not financial gain. If John were just a con man, would he suffer so much for his supposed beliefs? It doesn't seem likely.

John was participating with them not only in tribulation but also in the kingdom. He was experiencing the reign and rule of God with them right then in the present time. They experienced and celebrated God's rule in counter-cultural protest against other human rulers, political parties, and economic systems that demanded their allegiance. This combination of tribulation and kingdom explains the third thing listed: "patient endurance." John's own suffering demonstrates that there were no shortcuts or get-out-of-jail-free cards. Victory would only come through endurance.

John further describes how Jesus directly commissioned him to write: "Write therefore the things that you have seen, those that are and those that are to take place after this" (Rev 1:19). Some people take this verse as an outline for the book: the things that John had seen constitutes chapter 1, chapters 2–3 are the things that are, and chapters 4–22 are the things that must take place after this (generally understood to be the distant future, two thousand years or more after John wrote). Although such an approach might seem logical and attractive, it is misleading. The visions in Revelation 4–22 sometimes describe the past, often describe the present and immediate future, and only rarely describe the distant future. This is evident by the use of the phrase "after this." Gregory Beale convincingly argues that this phrase is a general way to describe the end times, which John and all the first Christians believed to have begun with Jesus's death and resurrection.[1] John stresses throughout that his visions would take place quickly and that the time was near (Rev 1:1, 3; 2:16; 3:11; 22:6, 7, 10, 12, 20). John was not wrong, and his visions began to be fulfilled right in the first century, even though the final fulfillment lay in the distant future.

THE REAL AUTHORITY

Although John presents himself as a legitimate and true prophet, he does not claim his own authority for his message. As we noted in the prior section, there is a clearly established chain of command from God to Jesus to an angel to John to the Christians. John points to God as the final authority for his message and the real

---

1. Beale, *The Book of Revelation*, 137–141, 152–170.

reason that the Christians needed to take it seriously. This is clear in the initial greetings in 1:4–5.

> John to the seven churches that are in Asia: Grace to you and peace from him who is and who was and who is to come, and from the seven spirits who are before his throne, and from Jesus Christ the faithful witness, the firstborn of the dead, and the ruler of kings on earth.

John identifies himself as the author but brings greetings from the Christian Triune God: the Father, the Spirit, and the Son. The Father is described as the one who is and who was and who is to come. These phrases focus not so much on eternal existence but on presence. God will not remain distant and remote forever but will one day physically and visibly come and dwell in his world. The Spirit is described as the seven spirits before God's throne. The description of the Spirit as seven-fold throughout Revelation (1:4; 3:1; 4:5; 5:6) is likely an allusion to Zechariah 4:2–7, where the seven lamps are identified as God's Spirit. The number seven in Revelation denotes fullness, completion, or cosmic order.

Jesus is described in three different ways in this initial greeting. He is (1) the faithful witness (2) who conquered death and (3) is currently reigning over the kings on earth. This is a startling claim since the first Christians were marginalized and poor, with no political power. Everyone knew the emperor ruled over the kings of the earth from Rome. John is here giving us God's perspective on reality: Jesus is the world's rightful ruler, despite the arrogant claims and threats of human rulers.

The rest of the chapter focuses on the power, majesty, and authority of Jesus. First, John guides us in worship of Jesus, the one who freed us from our sins and made us God's people, a kingdom of priests (1:5–6). Much like the book of Psalms in the Old Testament, the worship recounted in Revelation invites us to participate with John, the angels, and all of creation. The songs and expressions of worship throughout Revelation lead us into worship. You would do well to take John up on the implicit invitation, and when you read songs of worship in Revelation, slow down for a few moments and join in the cosmic celebration of our Creator and King.

Second, John recounts how Jesus appeared to him and commanded him to write to the seven churches in what is now western Turkey (1:11, 19). John is completely overwhelmed by the vision and falls down at Jesus's feet as though dead. John uses human language and metaphors drawn from the Old Testament (particularly Dan 7:9; 10:5–6) to try to describe to his hearers how Jesus appeared to him. Aspects of the vision, such as the white hair like wool, connect Jesus with the Ancient of Days in Daniel 7:9, and the cumulative effect of the details in the vision points to a powerful kingly and priestly figure. Aspects of the description are symbolic, such as the sword coming out of Jesus's mouth. The sword should be understood in light of Isaiah 11:4 and 49:2 as a powerful word of judgment against oppression and evil.

Revelation presents Jesus, alongside God, as the authority lying behind John's messages to the churches. Jesus is both terrifyingly powerful and good. When John falls down in terror, Jesus comforts him and tells him not to fear (1:17). Jesus then provides confidence to his people who may suffer and die for their faith: he conquered death and has the keys of Death and Hades (1:18). Death would not be victorious and had already been defeated! Further evidence of Jesus's goodness comes in the way that he loves us and freed us from our sins by his own blood (1:5). Jesus is a terrifyingly powerful authority figure, but he is good, and he has the best interests of his people in mind. Unlike human rulers, he sacrificed himself for the good of those under his authority.

CONCLUSION

The main function of Revelation 1 is to introduce and establish authority. John is merely a spokesperson for the world's rightful and true ruler. This ruler will not remain distant forever but will someday come to visibly and physically establish his rule in the world. The present time, however, is marked by conflict, suffering, and temptation. The world's rightful ruler has a message for his people to help them overcome and gain a victory in life that will reverberate throughout eternity. Revelation 1 answers the question posed in the beginning of this chapter: why should I listen, why should I obey, why should I care, why should I take Revelation seriously? Because God, the creator of the universe, has a message for you.

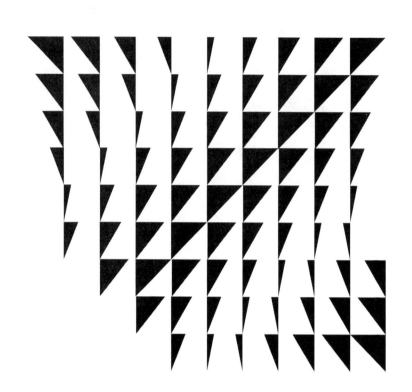

CHAPTER 7

Proclamations to Seven Churches

Revelation 1 ends with a vision of Jesus walking in the midst of seven lampstands, which symbolize seven churches in Asia Minor, modern-day western Turkey. This detail suggests presence; Jesus is not distant from his people. He is close to them. He knows their individual situations, their heartaches, their struggles, their strengths, and their sins. He also knows what they need to do to overcome and gain the victory in life.

Revelation 2–3 contains individual messages or proclamations from Jesus through John to each of these seven churches. The number seven was likely chosen because it represents completion or wholeness. The seven churches stand in for all the churches throughout the world and represent the strengths and weaknesses of all of God's people. Although each proclamation is specific to the original church in its specific city, John evidently intended all the churches to hear and respond to each of the messages. Jesus's comment about his judgment of the followers of Jezebel in the church of Thyatira makes this clear: "And all the churches will know that

I am he who searches mind and heart" (2:23). The proclamations were intended to be heard and responded to by every Christian. The seven proclamations all follow a similar format.

1. Each one is addressed to the angel of a particular church.

2. The speaker, Jesus, is then identified with a reference back to John's vision of Jesus in 1:12–16.

3. Jesus tells them something he knows about that particular church, whether good or bad.

4. This statement about reality is followed by encouragement or warnings, depending on the needs of the church.

5. The proclamation concludes with a call for spiritual discernment and a promise to the one who overcomes.

This consistent format would have made the original hearers think about imperial edicts, proclamations from the emperor. Imperial edicts would often begin with the phrase "thus says" along with a description of the emperor. They would then often have a statement of knowledge or an assessment of the situation followed by commendations and commands, with warnings against disobedience and promises for obedience. In addition to imperial edicts, the seven proclamations would also have caused some hearers to think about the Old Testament prophets, who often began their messages with "thus says the Lord." The messages of the Hebrew prophets generally provided God's perspective on their situation, encouragement to be faithful, and warning about future

Seeing the Big Picture

The seven proclamations enable Christians to gain God's perspective on reality and truth. They call God's people to repent if necessary and to overcome through obedience, perseverance, witness, and worship, despite the suffering they would surely endure.

judgment for disobedience. Most often, they called God's people to repentance for breaking the covenant.

These two backgrounds come together in the seven proclamations of Revelation 2–3. The proclamations present Jesus as speaking for God and as the true ruler of the world, in contrast to the Roman emperor. In the Old Testament, it is always God who introduces his messages with "thus says the Lord," and in Revelation, it is Jesus who speaks with that formulaic introduction. Both of these backgrounds highlight the authority and power of the speaker; these messages should not be ignored or dismissed! These are not suggestions from an annoying neighbor, unwanted advice from a relative, or requests from a door-to-door salesman; they are commands from the ruler of the kings of the earth.

In this chapter, we will briefly consider the five common parts of each of the proclamations.

THE CHURCH

Each proclamation is addressed to the angel of a particular church. These churches were located in Ephesus, Smyrna, Pergamum, Thyatira, Sardis, Philadelphia, and Laodicea. The proclamations are directed toward the angel connected to each of these churches. This puzzling detail is sometimes explained by noting that the Greek word for angel could simply mean "messenger" and might refer to the elder or human leader of each of these churches. This interpretation is not likely, however, because angels are referred to throughout Revelation and do not elsewhere refer to human beings. The more straightforward reading is that Christians in a particular geographical area have a heavenly angelic representative. This may seem strange to us today because the Western world has largely demythologized the universe, but ancient Jews and Christians had no hesitation about recognizing the reality of spiritual beings, both good and evil, both helpful and malicious, both serving God and opposing God. Even though the proclamation is directed toward the angel of each particular church, it is clear that the human beings in the church are the ones called on to respond.

THE SPEAKER

The speaker, Jesus, is then identified in each proclamation with a reference back to John's vision of Jesus in 1:12–16, reminding the hearers of the authority and power of the one speaking to them. Even though John is the one writing, it is not just John speaking to them. Some of the proclamations add details not contained in the original vision, such as the reference to Jesus having the "key of David" in 3:7 and being "the beginning [or ruler] of God's creation" in 3:14. This likely refers to Jesus, through his resurrection and victory over death, being the beginning of God's new creation or to his status as the ruler of God's creation.

JESUS'S KNOWLEDGE

Jesus proceeds to tell them something he knows about each church, whether good or bad. He provides God's assessment of them, an assessment that is not obvious on the surface of things. It is an assessment based on spiritual reality. The message is clear: you cannot hide from his gaze; you cannot deceive him; you cannot cover up your actions; you cannot blame others. We are good at fooling other people. We can put on a nice smile and spin reality in whatever way makes us look the best. But these proclamations make it crystal clear that Christ does not see things the way we do, and he cannot be fooled.

Consider three examples of how these proclamations function to give God's perspective on reality. First, Jesus says to the church in Smyrna in 2:9, "I know your tribulation and poverty (but you are rich)." From a human perspective, they were to be pitied. They were poor. They were marginalized and slandered by their broader society. They had no political power. They were suffering and living in poverty. They had nothing of value to offer. From a human perspective, that is all there was to the Christians in

Smyrna. God, however, sees things more clearly. He looks at them and does not see poverty, weakness, or helplessness. He declares them to be wealthy. They were suffering, but they were faithful. God views their faith in him as true wealth, a wealth that is far greater than their physical poverty.

In contrast to Smyrna, the Christians in Laodicea were wealthy. They were successful. They were respected. They seemed to have everything one could hope for in life. Jesus shares God's perspective in 3:17: "For you say, I am rich, I have prospered, and I need nothing, not realizing that you are wretched, pitiable, poor, blind, and naked." This contrast between Laodicea and Smyrna and between outward appearances and spiritual reality confronts us with a question: where is true wealth to be found? Revelation gives us God's perspective and invites us to live our lives based on what God values, what really matters and will last into eternity.

Second, Jesus makes it clear that the criterion for inclusion in God's people is not ethnicity but allegiance to him. There was evidently some kind of conflict between the Christian community of Jewish and gentile believers and some ethnic Jews in Philadelphia and Smyrna.

> I know your tribulation and your poverty (but you are rich) and the slander of those who say that they are Jews and are not, but are a synagogue of Satan. (2:9)

> Behold, I will make those of the synagogue of Satan who say that they are Jews and are not, but lie—behold, I will make them come and bow down before your feet, and they will learn that I have loved you. (3:9)

It seems that some ethnic Jews in these cities were slandering the Christians before the local authorities. Jesus declares that these particular ethnic Jews had lost the right to the name because of their rejection of him and opposition to his people. Salvation (for both ethnic Jews and gentiles) is determined by allegiance to Jesus and not by ethnicity.[1] Jesus makes it clear that ethnicity is neither a sufficient nor necessary reason to be included among God's people. To emphasize the severity of the loss that comes from rejecting him and opposing his people, Jesus takes prophecies of Israel's restoration from Isaiah (Isa 45:14; 49:23; 60:14) and applies them to the church in Philadelphia. In the original prophecies, gentiles are said to bow down before the feet of ethnic Israelites and acknowledge God's choice and blessing of Israel. In Revelation, the ethnic Jews who rejected Jesus are identified with the gentile nations, and the Christians (both Jews and gentiles) embody the identity of ethnic and national Israel in the restoration. This does not mean that gentile churches were replacing ethnic Israel. Instead, Jewish Christians represent and guarantee ethnic continuity with historic Israel, and gentile Christians are included in Israel's restoration through allegiance to Israel's king. These verses provide not a critique of Jews as Jews but rather a critique of some specific Jews who had allied with the dragon and beasts in opposition to Israel and her Messiah.

Third, Christ exposes the false teachers who were trying to convince Christians to compromise and blend in with the surrounding culture to avoid persecution and get ahead financially. These rival Christian teachers and prophets are described as those who hold to the teaching of Balaam (2:14), the Nicolaitans (2:15), and Jezebel, a particular prophetess active in the church of Thyatira (2:20-23); these different descriptions point to either one group or related groups holding similar positions. The main issues John raises are participation in the imperial cult (13:1-18), eating meat sacrificed to idols (2:14, 20), and sexual immorality (2:14, 20, 21; 9:21; 14:8; 17:2, 4; 18:3, 9; 19:2). John's references to sexual immorality likely refer to idolatry and false worship as spiritual adultery, but even if that is the case, idolatry was closely connected to actual sexual immorality

---

1. This conviction was widespread in early Christianity: Rom 2:29; 9:6; 2 Cor 1:20-21; Gal 3:29; 6:16; Eph 2:19; Phil 3:3-8; Tit 2:14; 1 Pet 1:1; 2:9.

in many cases. The Christians were experiencing significant social pressure to conform to societal expectations in these areas, and if they could just blend in a little better, they would have more social mobility and fewer problems.

John calls Christians to overcome through faithfulness even if it means the loss of prosperity and safety in this life. Other Christian leaders had the opposite message and tried to convince the Christians that prosperity and success in this life were possible if they were less strict, if the boundaries for overcoming behavior were not so high. The seven proclamations reveal God's perspective on the opposing teachers by connecting them with Balaam and Jezebel, wicked people in Israel's history who promoted idolatry and experienced God's judgment. The attractive message of compromise and prosperity becomes less attractive when viewed from God's perspective.

ENCOURAGEMENT OR WARNING

The statement concerning Jesus's knowledge of each church's spiritual reality is followed by encouragement or warning, depending on the needs of the church. An interesting pattern is present here. The middle three churches are mixed; they are filled with some Christians who are overcoming and victorious and others who are compromising and in danger of God's judgment. The second and sixth churches are not critiqued at all; they are described as healthy and victorious despite being the most oppressed, persecuted, and poor. The first and seventh churches are described as wholly compromised and completely in danger; the entire Ephesian church was in danger of having its lampstand removed, and the Laodicean Christians were about to be vomited out of Jesus's mouth. This literary pattern is called a chiasm. With such patterns, the center tends to be the most important, and I suggest that the center three churches reflect most of the churches globally and throughout history. Most churches are made up of some Christians seeking to be faithful and victorious in life through their faith and others who are compromising with sin and evil. Most churches are mixed and thus need to hear both warnings and assurances.

Christ calls compromising Christians in five of the churches to repent and provides severe warnings and threats to motivate repentance. In contrast, Christ calls faithful Christians to endure despite the intense suffering they were experiencing.

The two primary motivational strategies introduced in these seven proclamations recur throughout Revelation: there are promises centered on reward and eternal salvation for those who overcome and warnings about the judgment that accompanies failure to overcome. Both the promises and the warnings are directed toward the Christian hearers. These warnings are less about eternal security and election and more about assurance of salvation. How do people know that they are elect, that their conversion was genuine? In Revelation, Christians increase their assurance of salvation by responding to the warnings with repentance and perseverance.[2]

CONCLUDING PROMISE

Each proclamation ends with a call for the Christians to spiritually interpret the message and a promise to the one who overcomes. These promises are linked to the visions of resurrection life in God's new creation in Revelation 21-22 or to the visions of believers in victory and at rest throughout Revelation. All of God's promises are reserved for the one who overcomes (21:7).

CONCLUSION

Where do you stand today? With which church do you most identify, and which aspect of the message do you most need to hear? Many Christians today are familiar with the seven proclamations from Revelation 2-3 because these are the sections that preachers normally choose for sermon series. These passages are easier to understand and seem more directly and immediately applicable

---

2. This is similar to the logic of assurance expressed in 2 Peter 1:8-11.

than many of the later visions. Overfamiliarity, however, can often cause us to miss the force of the proclamations.

Often, churches have a view of themselves that is different from Christ's. Compromise with the world leads to ease and comfort, while faithful witness to Christ leads to persecution and difficulty. The seven proclamations seek to motivate us to overcome sin, evil, and temptation by warning us of the dangers of compromise and helping us see the eternal benefits of victory. It is clear that victory will involve suffering and sacrifice in the present time but will have eternal benefits. These seven short proclamations make the goal of Revelation clear. The visions help us see reality from God's perspective so that we can make difficult choices in the present time.

Without God's perspective, we quickly focus on what we can see with our eyes and touch with our hands. We focus on the immediate fulfillment of our desires, which often leads to sin and addiction and results in harm to ourselves and others. God's perspective, however, enables us to see beyond the present moment and beyond the physical realm. Jesus is always calling his churches back to faithfulness, repentance, and perseverance. This is the purpose of Revelation. It is not a detailed blueprint of end-time events but a powerful exhortation to the church to persevere in faithfulness to the end. May you have ears to hear and eyes to see what the Spirit is speaking to you today.

Warnings and Threats to Compromising Christians

Rev 2:5: Ephesus: "Remember therefore from where you have fallen; repent, and do the works you did at first. If not, I will come to you and remove your lampstand from its place, unless you repent."

Rev 2:16: Pergamum: "Therefore repent. If not, I will come to you soon and war against them with the sword of my mouth."

Rev 2:22: Thyatira: "Behold, I will throw her onto a sickbed, and those who commit adultery with her I will throw into great tribulation, unless they repent of her works."

Rev 3:3: Sardis: "Remember, then, what you received and heard. Keep it, and repent. If you do not wake up, I will come like a thief, and you will not know at what hour I will come against you."

Rev 3:16, 19: Laodicea: "I will spit you out of my mouth ... so be zealous and repent."

CHAPTER 8

The Heavenly Throne Room

REVELATION 4—5

J ohn sees and hears the content of Revelation 1-3 while he is on the island of Patmos. In chapter 4, John is called up in the Spirit to God's heavenly throne room. The spiritual realm is not all the same; it is not undifferentiated. In early Jewish and Christian thinking, the lowest heaven, as it were, is directly parallel to the created world, while the highest heaven is God's throne room, the holy of holies in the heavenly temple; that is where John is brought in this vision. We do not know if John was transported physically or just spiritually. When Paul recounts a similar experience in 2 Corinthians 12, he indicates that he himself did not know if it was in or out of the body.

> I know a man in Christ who fourteen years ago was caught up to the third heaven—whether in the body or out of the body I do not know, God knows. And I know that this man was caught up into paradise—whether in the body or out of the body I do not know, God knows—and he heard things that cannot be told, which man may not utter. (2 Cor 12:2-4)

John's experience in Revelation 4–5 is similar, except that he is commanded to write what he has seen and send it as a letter to the churches.

Seeing the Big Picture

- John's vision of God's throne in heaven assures believers of God's sovereignty and power and invites us to join in worship of our Creator.

- The vision of Jesus as a conquering Lion and slain Lamb describes his victory over evil through his sacrificial death and resurrection. Because of this cosmic victory over evil, he is able to complete God's plan for his creation: the defeat of evil through judgment and the transformation of the world into a new creation.

- These visions correspond to Jesus's ascension and enthronement in heaven following his physical resurrection.

GOD ON HIS THRONE

Who is really in charge of the universe? Who has real and final authority? The chaos of the world and of history forces this question. Evil so easily seems to win, despite our attempts to do right and advance justice. We can look around at the world and see problems everywhere. There are civil wars, assassinations, mass migrations, warnings of environmental collapse due to humanity's mismanagement of creation, fears of a global economic recession, fears of war, and fears of political upheaval. In the past century alone there have been two world wars and several instances of mass genocide.

When we look at the world with our physical eyes, it could seem that evil is winning. No matter how educated or skilled our political leaders are, they eventually mess things up through corruption or other moral failures. We cannot seem to fix ourselves as a human race, and our pursuit of unlimited entertainment and pleasure is undermining the moral stability of society. The future does not look bright, and it does not look like it is under control.

Later in Revelation, in chapters 12 and 13, we will encounter visions that show us the spiritual reality. Not only are we destroying ourselves through our own sin, but there are also active evil spiritual beings who are misleading, deceiving, and trying to destroy humanity. Before we are shown that vision, however,

Revelation 4 gives us a vision of who is truly in charge: God on his throne.

The throne is the center of the scene in Revelation 4, with something like concentric circles of attendants; the four living creatures are surrounded by the twenty-four elders, who are surrounded by thousands and thousands of angels.

The colors and sounds are vivid, beautiful, and overwhelming. Although John provides no physical description of God, the stones, colors, and sounds communicate God's splendor and power. The rainbow around the throne reminds us of Noah and of God's faithfulness to his promises to humanity. The four living creatures likely represent the created world. Their faces represent domesticated animals, wild animals, birds, and humans, and the number four is generally associated in Revelation with the created realm. Their appearance blends details attributed to cherubim and seraphim in prior prophetic visions in Isaiah and Ezekiel (Isa 6:2-3; Ezek 1:5-25). These spiritual beings are always closely connected to God and his throne. The twenty-four elders are likely spiritual representatives of God's people, similar to the angel associated with the church in each geographical area. The elders are clothed in white like God's people in other visions, and they are later described as holding bowls of incense, which represent the prayers of God's people (Rev 5:8). The number twenty-four could represent the unity of God's people between the Old and New Testaments—the twelve tribes of Israel and the twelve apostles— or, more likely, the twenty-four orders of priests who served in the temple (1 Chr 24:1-19).

Revelation 4 provides a foundation for all the visions to come in the book and for our lives today. Remembering principle 5 (read Revelation as Christian Scripture), we are drawn to reflect on the theological significance of the vision.

God is on his throne.

No matter what chaos you may be experiencing in your family or your job, God is on the throne.

No matter what sickness you may be fighting, God is on the throne.

No matter what sin you may be struggling with, God is on the throne.

No matter what fears you may have about the future, God is on the throne.

No matter how much money you have, or don't have, in the bank, God is on the throne.

No matter how hard life might get, God is on the throne.

This is the foundational vision God gave John to share with us.

God is on the throne, and there is no force in the universe capable of defeating him or wresting control from him.

WORSHIP

Revelation 4's vision of God on his throne leads to worship. In worship, we draw our attention away from ourselves, away from our weaknesses, away from our fears and insecurities, away from our problems. Worship directs our attention to God, the Creator and Sustainer of the universe, our Protector and Provider. The hymns of worship in Revelation are included to draw us into worship. They are there not just to give us information about what some angels are doing in heaven but to invite us to join in the rightful worship given by creation to the Creator.

We need to worship, and we will worship. We were created to worship, and if we do not worship God, we will find ourselves worshipping idols. Empty pursuits, empty goals, and empty desires leave us empty and unsatisfied. Every human being worships; the question is what they worship. As Christians, we worship the Creator of the universe, and proper worship helps everything else in life fall into its proper place. False worship keeps life out of balance, but true worship brings stability and wholeness. The worship and pursuit of idols diminishes life, while the worship of the true

God infuses life with meaning and purpose. Worship calms our hearts and helps us see reality from God's perspective.

The two hymns recorded in Revelation 4 are short and simple. The hymn in verse 8 celebrates the holiness of God, his uniqueness and separateness. God's holiness by itself produces fear because we are not holy. We are not worthy to draw near to God or exist in his presence. If God's holiness can be described as a consuming fire, we are like dried-out Christmas trees in January; one spark leads to an instant bonfire. The next chapter shows us why God's holiness is not a cause of fear for God's people: the Lamb is worthy! We are not worthy, but the Lamb's blood covers our sins, and we join with him in his worthiness. Because of Jesus, we can draw near and worship a holy God without fear. The hymn also reminds us that we worship a God who was and is and is to come. This expresses not just our faith in God's eternal existence but also our hope in the future. God is not only eternally existent; he is also coming to his creation. He will not remain distant and invisible forever but will one day come physically, materially, and visibly to his creation. He is the one who is to come.

The hymn in verse 11 celebrates God's worthiness to receive our worship. A simple reason is given: he created everything that exists. When we worship, we are drawing near to the one who spoke us into existence. God's role as Creator also establishes another important point: the one who has the power to create also has the power and right to de-create and re-create. The visions in Revelation show a process of de-creation that leads to the removal of evil and the inbreaking of a new creation. Looking to God's activity as Creator in the past gives us confidence regarding his ability to create a new future.

These hymns, along with the other songs of worship throughout Revelation, can serve as examples for us in our own worship, and many of our worship songs are based on the hymns of Revelation.

They invite us to join the hosts of heaven and all of creation in worship of the world's rightful and true Ruler.

THE VICTORIOUS LION AND SLAIN LAMB

Revelation 5 contains one of the most significant scenes in the whole book. First, John sees a scroll in God's hand, filled with writing on both sides but sealed with seven seals. The scroll likely represents God's plan to rescue his people, judge evil, and bring his creation to its goal. No one, however, is found worthy to open the scroll and carry out God's plans. No human being or spiritual being in all of creation is worthy to open the scroll. This reality leads John to weep because it effectively means that evil will triumph and God's creation will remain deformed, disordered, and chaotic forever.

John's tears are interrupted by one of the elders. "And one of the elders said to me, 'Weep no more; behold, the Lion of the tribe of Judah, the Root of David, has conquered, so that he can open the scroll and its seven seals' " (5:5). John *hears* a description of someone who is worthy. This individual is the Lion connected to the tribe of Judah in ancient prophecy (Gen 49:8-12) and the descendant (root) of David promised by God in Isaiah (Isa 11:1-10). John *hears* that this Lion has overcome or gained the victory and is able to open the scroll and its seals.

John *looks and sees* a Lamb next to the throne, standing as though slain, with seven horns symbolizing power and seven eyes identified as the seven spirits of God. The Lamb has obviously been slaughtered but is just as obviously alive again. This is a clear example of a literary device John uses throughout Revelation whereby he tells us first what he hears and then what he sees. Generally, what he hears and what he sees are opposite and would not normally be identified together. This clash of expectations guides us as readers to reflect on the significance of describing a slain but living lamb as a conquering lion.

The conquering Lion helps us recognize this figure as the Messiah promised throughout the Old Testament and affirms that God's Messiah has won and conquered evil. The slain Lamb shows us how he conquered evil. He conquered by being conquered, by being faithful to the point of death on the cross. The image of the Lamb also connects back to sacrificial imagery and the sacrificial system of the Old Testament. The blood of the Lamb is connected to our salvation, victory, and freedom from sin at several points in Revelation (1:5; 5:9; 7:14; 12:11). The Passover lamb, in particular, provides a close parallel since several of the judgments described in Revelation have intentional parallels to the exodus judgments.

This vision reveals that God's victory over evil comes first not through violent judgment against evil people and spiritual beings but through sacrificially experiencing violence to rescue people from sin and evil. God is not aloof and uninterested in our suffering but experienced pain and sorrow alongside us. He entered into a broken world and experienced the worst evil, shame, and suffering possible. He absorbed it and came out victorious over it. He then shares his victory with those who follow him in the way of victory: faithful witness, worship, and obedience to the point of death.

Isaiah 53 vividly describes the significance of the Lamb slain for us and on our behalf.

> Surely he has borne our griefs and carried our sorrows; yet we esteemed him stricken, smitten by God, and afflicted. But he was pierced for our transgressions; he was crushed for our iniquities; upon him was the chastisement that brought us peace, and with his wounds we are healed. All we like sheep have gone astray; we have turned—every one—to his own way; and the LORD has laid on him the iniquity of us all. He was oppressed, and he was afflicted, yet he opened not his mouth; like a lamb that is led to the slaughter, and like a sheep that before its shearers is silent, so he opened not his mouth. (Isa 53:4–7)

When the Lamb takes the scroll, the spiritual beings around the throne sing a new song declaring the Lamb to be worthy to take and open the scroll because of his sacrificial death. The Lamb is worthy to bring God's plan to fulfillment because his death purchased people for God from every tribe, language, people, and nation (Rev 5:9). This short hymn of worship refers back to God's original plan for rescuing Israel from Egypt as stated in Exodus 19:6, to make them a kingdom of priests. This has finally been fulfilled in the multiethnic group of people who have been ransomed by the Lamb's blood. The hymn closes by celebrating the future of God's people: "they shall reign on the earth" (Rev 5:10). This refers not just to the purpose for rescuing Israel from Egypt but also to God's original purpose for creating humanity. In Genesis 1:26–28, God commands human beings, as his image-bearing representatives, to fill and subdue the earth—in essence, to represent him and carry his presence throughout his creation. The Lamb's blood has ransomed a people from every ethnicity and nation to fulfill God's original plan for humanity!

After this initial hymn, the four living creatures and twenty-four elders are joined by a massive number of angels in another song of worship declaring the worthiness of the Lamb. The word "myriad" indicates ten thousand, so the phrase "myriads of myriads" can be translated as ten thousands times ten thousands. The goal with such a numerical description is not to provide us with an exact number but to poetically express the magnitude of the number. There were a whole lot of angels participating in worship.

This massive group is expanded for the final hymn of Revelation 5 to include "every creature in heaven and on earth and under the earth and in the sea, and all that is in them." This poetically expresses the totality of the created order. As a prophetic scene of anticipation, it is a crescendo of worship that is produced by all of God's creation in celebration of the Lamb's victorious death and resurrection. This hymn is particularly important because it includes both God and the Lamb together in cosmic worship:

"To him who sits on the throne and to the Lamb" (5:13). Later in Revelation, John is strictly rebuked for worshipping angels because angels, like humans, are created beings (19:10; 22:8). The Lamb, however, does not fit in this category but is included with God as the only rightful recipients of worship. This is not an explicit statement about the Trinity, but it certainly points in that direction.

CONCLUSION

The throne room vision of Revelation 4–5 provides the theological foundation and center for all the visions to come. No matter what terrifying things lie ahead, we can move forward convinced and assured that God is on his throne. He is ruling and reigning over his creation. In addition, we have confidence that Jesus's death and resurrection gained a cosmic victory over evil, and Jesus, now ruling and reigning at God's right hand in heaven, is able to put God's plan into action.

John's sorrow at the possibility that evil might continue unchecked in God's creation forever is replaced with confidence that the victory of the Lamb will lead to the fulfillment of God's plan for his creation. There are no explicit chronological markers in the vision to indicate exactly when this happened, but it is likely that John sees the results in heaven of Jesus's ascension and enthronement. This is suggested by the hymn in 5:9–10, which looks to Jesus's death in the past and the reign of believers on the earth in the future; the time is thus the present. John's present in the first century is, of course, our past, but we have not yet reached the end with Jesus's second coming. The events happening in God's throne room in Revelation 4–5 thus took place in history around AD 30 or 33 (depending on when one dates the crucifixion).

Chapter 5 ends with a cliff-hanger. The Lamb is in possession of God's scroll, and all of creation is celebrating and worshiping. The reader is not left in suspense for long; the Lamb immediately begins to open the seals.

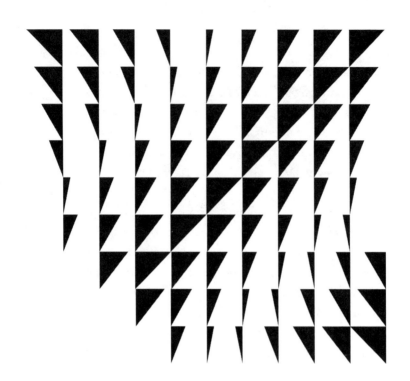

CHAPTER 9

The Seven Seals

U p to this point in Revelation, many people agree on the main points. With the opening of the first seal in Revelation 6, however, various interpretive approaches come to very different conclusions. I don't want to understate or overstate the difficulty. The visions can be difficult to understand, and there are many interpretive options, but the big picture is generally quite clear. The five principles discussed in Part 1 provide the keys for reading John's visions: they are highly symbolic, engage in frequent repetition, and would have been largely understandable to the first hearers.

THE FOUR HORSEMEN: REVELATION 6:1—8

Jesus immediately begins opening the seven seals. Each of the first four seals is connected to a particular horseman. Thanks to many references in movies and the media, the four horsemen of the Apocalypse are perhaps the most widely recognized vision of Revelation. Even though each horseman comes at the command of one of the four living creatures, the four horsemen are presented as destructive evil forces. God allows evil spiritual forces to fulfill their purposes as a form of judgment against evil humanity.

The first horseman is connected to human warfare and conquest, the second to civil unrest and civil wars, and the third to famine (the prices listed for basic food are eight to sixteen times the average); the fourth, death, functions as a summary of the whole group. The inclusion of death as the final, summarizing horseman indicates the demonic character of all four, since death is presented throughout Revelation as a personified evil figure whom Christ conquered through his resurrection and who would finally be cast into the lake of fire. Even though death is presented as God's adversary, it is under his control. The four horsemen function together as a unified destructive group, so even though the first horseman rides a white horse, has a crown, and conquers in a way similar to Jesus in Revelation 19:11–16, this is not Jesus.

These four horsemen represent the warfare, chaos, and suffering that take place throughout history. Many interpreters connect the four horsemen with Jesus's teaching in the Olivet Discourse: "And you will hear of wars and rumors of wars. See that you are not alarmed, for this must take place, but the end is not yet. For nation will rise against nation, and kingdom against kingdom, and there will be famines and earthquakes in various places. All these are but the beginning of the birth pains" (Matt 24:6–8; see the parallels in Mark 13:7–9; Luke 21:9–12). Wars, rumors of wars, famines, and earthquakes do

---

Seeing the Big Picture

- Revelation 6:1–8:5 provides an overview of history from Jesus's enthronement until his second coming.

- The first four seals take place within history as human beings experience the consequences of their own evil.

- The fifth seal shows a response from God's people, who experience suffering and persecution as history unfolds.

- The sixth and seventh seals describe the end, the great day of God's final judgment.

- The sealing of the 144,000 communicates God's ownership and protection of his people in the midst of the chaos and evil of history, the great tribulation.

not indicate the end but represent the upheavals of history that would precede the end. The metaphor of birth pains could suggest that things will intensify and get worse as we get closer to the end.

Similar to Jesus's teaching, John's vision presents the four horsemen as active throughout human history, beginning with Jesus's enthronement at God's right hand. They are not special events reserved for a period right before Jesus returns, but rather, they represent the chaos of history as a form of God's judgment of the world. How should we make sense of this theologically? Is God to blame for the many innocent deaths that occur through human conflict?

Since Revelation should be read as Christian Scripture (principle 5), a comparison with Romans 1 is helpful at this point. Paul makes the astounding claim that God's wrath is being revealed (in the present tense) on ungodly and unrighteous people who suppressed the truth of God (Rom 1:18). When Paul goes on to describe how God's punishment is being revealed in history, he does not mention active judgment of any kind. Rather, he says, God hands humanity over to its own sinful choices. Human beings choose to reject God and pursue evil, and God judges them by allowing them to do as they please. This permissive judgment leads to greater sin and the natural self-destruction caused by sin. Paul does believe that God will finally judge all of humanity at the end of time, but he describes God's judgment of sin in the present time as God handing people over to the consequences of their own choices. John's apocalyptic visions make the same point. God's judgment in history largely consists of allowing people to pursue their own sin, their own pride, and their own lust. The free exercise of human free will leads, regularly and repeatedly, to conflict and human suffering. The suffering is not directly caused by God but is a result of God handing us over to the consequences of our own actions.

The first readers would have easily identified points of fulfillment already taking place in the first century as Roman conquests led to civil unrest (particularly in AD 69) and famine (particularly in AD 92). The vision helps Christians interpret the present time as a time of chaos and judgment. But this chaos is not arbitrary or pointless; God is moving history forward toward its goal.

THE FIFTH SEAL: REVELATION 6:9—11

Christians also suffer through history alongside non-Christians. We share in sickness, natural disasters, and the terrible consequences of human conflict and oppression. Christians are not magically immune from suffering, and, as the later visions in Revelation make clear, we will actually suffer even more than most people because of our faithfulness to Jesus.

When the Lamb opens the fifth seal, nothing happens in history; nothing moves forward in the narrative. Time stands still, and John sees a vision of God's people who have suffered and been killed for their faithful witness calling out to God to bring justice to the earth. Jesus often described discipleship as an embrace of death when he called people to take up their cross and follow him. This could suggest that this vision of God's victorious people includes both those who were literally killed for their faith and those who faithfully followed Jesus in daily bearing the cross of self-sacrificial discipleship.

This is a vision of God's people in the intermediate state between death and resurrection life in God's new creation. They are pictured as alert and active, not asleep. They are at rest and clothed with white robes symbolizing victory. The souls are described as under the altar, and, although it is not explicit, this is likely the altar of incense in the heavenly temple. Throughout Revelation, incense is connected to the prayers of God's people, and here they are pictured as praying for God to act and bring just judgment. The call for God to avenge should be understood not as a longing for excessive or spiteful punishment (he hurt me, so I want to hurt him) but rather as a longing for justice, for God to set right everything that is wrong in the world. The haunting question "How long?" is a common cry throughout biblical laments. We often don't understand and can't easily explain why God allows evil in the world to continue and his people to suffer. We long for Jesus to return and transform God's world into his promised new creation.

The message from God to them alerts us to the fact that more Christians would suffer and die for their witness before the end. The idea that a certain number of people needed to be born or killed before the end was common in contemporary Jewish apocalyptic books (1 Enoch 47:1-4; 4 Ezra 4:33-37; 2 Baruch 21:19-23; 23:4-7). We could also perhaps recognize a parallel with God's words to Abraham about the land in Genesis 15:16. The wickedness of the inhabitants had not yet reached the point where God would act in judgment, but that time would come in the future. When the wickedness of the Amorites became complete, God would act in judgment to destroy them and replace them in the land with the Israelites. Such action is presented not as arbitrary or genocidal but as judgment of evil. The slaughter and persecution of innocent people by evil people will eventually reach a point of no return, a point at which God will act; oppression will not go on unchecked forever.

We may not understand why God delays, and we may regularly cry out to God "How long?"; but we are called to trust that when he acts, it will be at the right time and will be just. Justice may seem delayed, but it will come. Laments like this are not a sign of unbelief or lack of confidence in God. They rather give voice to our suffering and are motivated by our faith in a God who has promised to bring ultimate justice: to save the righteous and judge evil. The vision of the fifth seal is crucial for the visions that follow because it presents God's judgment of the world as a response to the prayers of his people for justice.

THE SIXTH SEAL: REVELATION 6:12—17

In contrast to the lack of action in the fifth seal, with the opening of the sixth seal, all Hell seems to break loose. The vision describes complete cosmic upheaval and universal fear and panic. The language closely matches Jesus's description in the Olivet Discourse of the cosmic upheaval that would accompany the coming of the Son of Man.

Revelation 6:12–14	Mark 13:24–26
There was a great earthquake, and the sun became black as sackcloth, the full moon became like blood, and the stars of the sky fell to the earth as the fig tree sheds its winter fruit when shaken by a gale. The sky vanished like a scroll that is being rolled up, and every mountain and island was removed from its place.	But in those days, after that tribulation, the sun will be darkened, and the moon will not give its light, and the stars will be falling from heaven, and the powers in the heavens will be shaken. And then they will see the Son of Man coming in clouds with great power and glory.

This language of cosmic upheaval is regularly used by the Old Testament prophets to describe God's judgments of Babylon, Edom, Egypt, and even Israel (Isa 13:10–13; 34:4; Ezek 32:6–8; Joel 2:10, 30–31; Hab 3:6–11). The prophets generally use images of cosmic upheaval to figuratively describe the destruction of cities and nations by human armies within history. We do something similar today when we speak of earthshaking news or events that turn our world upside down. It is thus impossible to know how literally we should interpret this language of cosmic upheaval. Throughout Revelation, language of cosmic upheaval is used to describe the events of the end that are associated with the final judgment and Jesus's return (16:18–20; 20:11). It may not be literal in every sense, but the imagery pictures a de-creation that makes way for a new creation.

The list of people affected shows that the final judgment levels humanity. Social status doesn't provide an advantage. Every human being, from the kings of the earth to the lowliest slaves, must give an account to a God who shows no favoritism based on wealth, status, or ethnicity.

The language here is so extreme and so devastating that it appears the final end has come. In addition, the people describe it as the great day of the wrath of God and the Lamb (Rev 6:17). The "day of the Lord" is a common phrase used throughout the Old Testament prophets to describe either moments of God's judgment within history or a final and climactic day of judgment and salvation. In the Hebrew prophets, the day of the Lord always includes both the judgment of evil people and the salvation of God's faithful people. The description of this day in Revelation as belonging to both God and the Lamb closely connects Jesus to God. Despite the fact that we have reached the end in the narrative with the sixth seal, there are still many more visions to come in Revelation. Many of the upcoming visions bring us back in time and provide different perspectives and details on the period between Jesus's first and second comings.

Chapter 6 ends with a question: Who can stand in the day of the Lord (v. 17)? Who is able to survive it?

REVELATION 7: THE 144,000 FROM ISRAEL AND THE UNCOUNTABLE MULTITUDE FROM EVERY NATION

Revelation 7 answers the question that closes chapter 6. Who is able to stand in the day of the wrath of God? The visions in chapter 7 answer this question by going back in time to before the first seal was opened. John sees four angels holding back the four winds of the earth. These "four winds" are destructive forces that will bring harm to the earth, the sea, and the trees. They connect forward to the first two trumpets in Revelation 8, which target the earth, trees, and sea, and they connect backward to the four horsemen. The connection to the four horsemen is not so obvious but becomes clear through considering the four sets of horses in the visions of Zechariah. Zechariah saw a vision of four chariots pulled by red, black, white, and dappled horses (Zech 6:1–8). The Greek version of the Old Testament, which John likely used, makes it clear that the four chariots were the four winds of heaven (Zech 6:5). This suggests a close connection, if not identification, between the four horsemen of Revelation 6:1-8 and the four winds of 7:1 and helps us see that this sealing of God's people took place before the sealed scroll began to be opened.

Before receiving an answer to the question "Who can stand?" John is shown a vision of something God did before any of the seals were opened: he sealed his people on their foreheads. Revelation 14:1 reveals that this seal was the name of Jesus and God written on their foreheads. Paul regularly connects God's seal on people with the Holy Spirit (2 Cor 1:22; Eph 1:13; 4:30), but John does not make this connection in Revelation. The Old Testament background for God's seal in Revelation can be found in Ezekiel 9:1-7, in which Ezekiel receives a vision about God's judgment of Jerusalem for idolatry and injustice. He sees a man in linen who places a mark on those who are faithful in Jerusalem, while other men come behind and slay all who do not have God's mark. God's seal in both Revelation and Ezekiel communicates ownership and protection. Those who are sealed will not experience God's wrath. This is proved by the fact that the demonic locusts in Revelation 9:4 are not allowed to afflict those with God's seal. It does not provide protection, however, from the wrath of the dragon in chapter 12, who empowers two beasts to kill those who will not receive the mark (name) of the beast on their foreheads (Rev 13:15). God's seal and the beast's mark are set in explicit contrast to each other in Revelation.

John "heard the number of the sealed, 144,000, sealed from every tribe of the sons of Israel" (7:4). John then hears a listing of the twelve tribes (7:5-8). If we remember the difference in chapter 5 between what John heard (a lion) and what he saw (a lamb), it may be natural to wonder about what John will see based upon what he just heard. He tells us immediately: "After this I looked, and behold, a great multitude that no one could number, from every nation, from all tribes and peoples and languages, standing before the throne and before the Lamb, clothed in white robes, with palm branches in their hands" (Rev 7:9).

John *hears* that a limited and countable number of ethnic Israelites would be sealed, and then he *sees* an uncountable number of people from every ethnicity standing before the throne and before the Lamb. What he hears and what he sees are contradictory, and this has led to a great deal of discussion regarding the relationship of the 144,000 Israelites to the uncountable multitude from every nation. John's visions often contain a dramatic shift between what he hears and what he subsequently sees. Another example is in Revelation 21:9. He hears that he is about to see the bride of the Lamb, but what he sees is the heavenly Jerusalem coming down from heaven (21:10). Is it the bride or is it a city? The city is the bride.

John uses this hearing/seeing literary technique at crucial points in the visions to force us to consider how two opposite realities are essentially the same. The Lion is the Lamb, the bride is the city, and the 144,000 Israelites are an uncountable multiethnic multitude. Together, the visions of chapter 7 enable us to answer the question with which chapter 6 ended. Who is able to stand in the great day of the Lord? Those who have been sealed by God with his name on their forehead will be the ones able to stand in that day.

Even if the 144,000 are closely connected to the innumerable multitude, the different perspectives are important and should not be ignored. The number 144,000 is symbolic and results from multiplying 12 by 12 by 1,000. The number points toward the joining of the twelve tribes of Israel with the twelve apostles and the resultant multiplication. We will see more multiples of twelve in the vision of the New Jerusalem in Revelation 21, and the number twelve in Revelation indicates the completed people of God. The way the tribes are listed suggests that they are being counted in a census in preparation for warfare (see Num 1). God's people are thus pictured as an army sealed by God's name and prepared to engage in conflict. Several of the visions throughout Revelation use the imagery of holy war, but it is a war fought with witness, worship, and obedience and not with physical weapons. The 144,000 describe God's people who are about to suffer and be tempted in the battle to overcome.

The uncountable multitude, on the other hand, have come through the conflict. They have suffered and borne faithful witness. They "are the ones coming out of the great tribulation" who "have washed their robes and made them white in the blood of the Lamb" (Rev 7:14). They are pictured in the intermediate state between death and resurrection life in God's new creation. They are in the throne room worshipping and celebrating. The vision of believers in victory and at rest in 7:9–17 parallels the short description of souls under the altar in the fifth seal (6:9–11) and also has many connections to later visions of God's people in victory and at rest.

Some interpreters connect the reference to a "great tribulation" with a literal seven-year period of intense suffering that is supposedly going to take place right before Jesus returns. The problem is that John does not say any of that, and for John, the tribulation had already started in the first century and would characterize all the time until Jesus returned. Recall that John describes himself as a partner in *tribulation* with the churches (1:9), the Christians in Smyrna were already experiencing *tribulation* and would continue to experience it (2:9–10), and God's judgment of those who followed false teaching in the church in Thyatira is described as "*great tribulation*" (2:22). *The phrase "great tribulation" in Revelation is not a technical phrase that refers to a seven-year period, but rather, it describes the entire period of time between Jesus's resurrection and second coming as a time of great tribulation.* This is in line with the rest of the New Testament, which views tribulation as a present reality for God's people.[1]

---

1. See the references to tribulation (*thlipsis*) in Matt 13:21; 24:9; Mark 4:17; John 16:33; Acts 11:19; 14:22; 20:23; Rom 5:3; 8:35; 12:12; 2 Cor 1:4, 8; 4:17; 6:4; 8:2; Col 1:24; 1 Thess 1:6; 3:3; 2 Thess 1:4; Heb 10:33.

The two contrasting images in Revelation 7 thus show God's people before entering into deadly conflict on the one hand and after coming out of it on the other. Apart from offering their different perspectives, the contrasting images point to the same fundamental reality. The 144,000 who are sealed figuratively represent all of God's people between the first and second comings of Christ. Several other clues in Revelation point to this interpretation. The 144,000 are described as *servants* of God (7:3) and as those who have been *ransomed from the earth* (14:3–4), and both of these descriptions are used elsewhere in Revelation to describe all of God's people and not just a special sub-set (1:1; 2:20; 5:9; 19:5; 22:3). We have already seen that John ascribes a Jewish identity to God's people in the present time even though non-Jewish believers were being included in Israel's restoration. This is evident in how he describes God's multiethnic people as a kingdom of priests, in fulfillment of Exodus 19:6, and as true Israel in 2:9 and 3:9. Descriptions of God's multiethnic people as the twelve tribes of Israel fit with John's view of God's people as Israel (Jewish believers in Jesus with gentile Christians included). This is confirmed by how John alludes to God's promise to Abraham to give him uncountable descendants when he describes the multiethnic multitude "that no one could number" (7:9). Finally, the list of the twelve tribes does not match any lists from the Old Testament. It is a fundamentally theological list. Judah is at the front of the list, even though he was not the firstborn in order, to highlight the fact that the Messiah came from the tribe of Judah; it is thus a messianically focused list. Levi is included because God's people are described as priests throughout Revelation. Dan and Ephraim are excluded (to make room for Levi and Joseph) because those two tribes were most associated with idolatry in Israel's history. The shape of the list of tribes, therefore, further supports its symbolic meaning.

THE SEVENTH SEAL: REVELATION 8:1, 3—5

After describing who would be able to stand in the great day of God's future wrath in Revelation 7, John returns to narrate the opening of the seventh seal. At first, nothing seems to happen, and there is silence in heaven for half an hour. This silence, however, is filled with meaning. First, silence is often associated with judgment in the Old Testament prophets, and Paul describes how every mouth will be silenced before God at the final judgment because there will be nothing that could be said in their defense (Rom 3:19). Second, in contemporary Jewish writings, silence in heaven was associated with the prayer of God's people. All of heaven becomes silent to symbolically ensure that God hears prayer. The souls under the altar prayed for God to act in judgment, and the silence of the seventh seal confirms that God hears their prayer. This connection between the fifth and seventh seals is confirmed by what happens next. An angel stands by the altar (presumably the same altar mentioned in the fifth seal) and offers incense along with the prayers of the saints. The incense symbolizes the sweet-smelling nature of prayer; the prayers of God's people bring God pleasure. The seventh seal concludes with the angel taking fire from the altar and casting it in judgment on the earth. This action is accompanied by "peals of thunder, rumblings, flashes of lightning, and an earthquake." This description confirms for us that the seventh seal has ended since a similar description accompanies the ends of the seventh trumpet and seventh bowl judgments (compare Rev 8:5 with 11:19; 16:18).

The seventh seal doesn't move the narrative along but simply provides another perspective on the final judgment, which had already been narrated in the sixth seal's description of the day of the Lord. This new perspective is the connection between God's judicial actions and the prayer of his people for justice on the earth.

Some interpreters argue that the seven trumpets are the content of the seventh seal because they are introduced in Revelation 8:2, between the opening of the seventh seal in 8:1 and its conclusion in 8:3-5. This is a possible explanation, but the alternating topics more likely reflect a literary device John uses to link different visions. This is confirmed by the similar introduction to the bowl judgments in chapter 15. John introduces the seven angels with seven bowls in 15:1 but then uses 15:2-4 to conclude the prior topic before returning to the seven bowls in 15:5. John interlocks the seal and trumpet judgments in chapter 8 similarly.

CONCLUSION

The scroll sealed with seven seals represents God's plan to bring justice to the world and salvation to his people. Revelation 6:1-8:5 provides an overview of history from Jesus's enthronement until his second coming. The first four seals represent the chaos and suffering of history as human beings harm each other in their rebellion against God. The fifth seal shows us that God's people also suffer intense and fatal persecution during this time. They cry out for God to act and avenge the blood of unjust persecution. The sixth seal reveals the cosmic upheaval associated with the final day of the Lord, and the seventh seal makes it clear that God's judgments are the right response to the prayer of his people for justice.

The close connection between chapters 6 and 7 presents a contrast between those who are not able to stand in the day of the Lord (Christ's return and final salvation and judgment) and those who are able to stand in that day. This contrast functions to motivate us as readers to be part of the second group—don't compromise, remain faithful unto death, be part of the innumerable multitude and not the inhabitants of the earth who will experience God's judgment. Overcome! The vision gives us assurance that we are sealed with God's name; we are spiritually protected and will not experience his wrath.

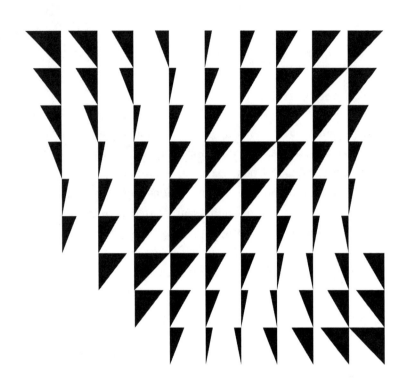

CHAPTER 10

The Seven Trumpets

The first six trumpets will likely produce a strong urge within you to try to read the details of the visions as literal descriptions of things that will take place at the end of history. It may seem natural to read them that way, but remember principle 4: recognize symbolism. Apocalyptic visions are not the same as historical narratives or literal future predictions. A key goal in ancient apocalyptic literature is to communicate the main points in a vivid, striking, memorable, and emotionally moving way. Many of the details in apocalyptic visions are primarily decorative and function to stir our emotions or cause us to reflect on Old Testament passages that have similar ideas and details. The goal is to read this literature in line with how the original author intended and as the first readers would have understood it—in line with the expectations of the apocalyptic genre.

THE SEVEN TRUMPETS

The big picture is relatively clear: the seven trumpets describe a series of judgments that intensify and culminate in the final judgment. However, this big picture doesn't answer all our questions, and we are confronted with the interpretive equivalent of a fork in the road. *Do these trumpet visions work the same way as the first four seals and describe God's judgments that began with Jesus's resurrection and occur throughout human history, or do they describe a particularly intense period of judgment right before the end?* This is not an easy question to answer, but the good news is that it doesn't really matter. It doesn't impact any significant point of Christian theology, and it doesn't change the original purpose of the book as a whole (remember principle 1: focus on the original purpose of the visions).

Having said that, there are good reasons to view the first six trumpets as roughly parallel to the four horsemen of the first four seals. They describe the chaos and evil of history as a form of God's judgment of evil as he allows human beings to experience the consequences of their own choices and evil spiritual forces to torment and afflict those who have rejected and rebelled against him. The first six trumpets provide a spiritual perspective and theological interpretation of the suffering of history.

This approach to the trumpets is supported by a detail that is easy to miss. Near the end of Revelation, John records a severe warning: "I warn everyone who hears the words of the prophecy of this book: if anyone adds to them, God will add to him the *plagues* described in this book" (22:18). This warning applied to the first hearers and every subsequent reader throughout history. The warning threatens that those who tamper with the book will experience the *plagues* recorded in the book. The first references to plagues in Revelation come in the sixth trumpet (9:18, 20).

Seeing the Big Picture

- The seven trumpet judgments give us a different perspective and different details on the period of time between Jesus's first and second comings. The seventh trumpet concludes at the final judgment.

- The visions of the temple and two witnesses between the sixth and seventh trumpets help Christians understand their identity and purpose during this same period. They are witnesses who will be spiritually protected while also being physically vulnerable.

The word is also used to describe how the two witnesses affect the world and their hearers (11:6). Most significantly, all seven of the final bowl judgments are repeatedly described as plagues (15:1, 6, 8; 16:9, 21; 21:9). The judgment of Babylon is also described as plagues (18:4, 8). Of these references, the sixth trumpet and the seven bowls are most likely the plagues threatened against those who might tamper with the book in 22:18. Those people will experience the plagues described in Revelation right then, not just at the end of history. If it is possible for people throughout history to be afflicted by the sixth trumpet and seven bowls, then it is likely that these judgments describe, with various symbolic details, God's judgments that are carried out throughout history.

If the trumpets largely parallel the seals and describe God's judgments throughout history, what is their unique contribution or perspective? Here are four points to consider.

1. While the first four seals focused on human warfare, civil unrest, famine, and disease, the trumpets largely focus on demonic spiritual oppression. This is particularly clear with regard to the fifth and sixth trumpets, which describe oppressive and murderous demons as grotesque, monstrous beasts. The demonic locusts of the fifth trumpet cause mental, emotional, and physical torment, while the demonic horses of the sixth trumpet wound and kill. The fallen star of the third trumpet likely points to a demonic being, in line with how fallen stars were understood in contemporary apocalyptic literature.

2. While both believers and unbelievers are affected by the human warfare described in the seals, the demonic oppression of the trumpets is explicitly directed toward those who do not have God's seal (9:4) and who are engaged in idolatrous worship, murder,

sexual immorality, and thefts (9:20-21). These plagues
are not pictured as randomly afflicting everyone but
are focused on people who are corrupted by sin and
are actively engaged in evil activities.

3. The first four trumpets use the imagery of ecological disaster. This could point to the ecological harm
that human beings cause themselves through their
mismanagement of creation, although this interpretation would not likely have occurred to the first
readers. More likely, the ecological focus of the first
four trumpets draws on the exodus plague traditions
along with other Old Testament descriptions of God
being involved in holy war. God is often pictured as
engaging in warfare in judgment of his enemies using
natural phenomena. The descriptions of God's use of
nature in holy war are normally literal in historical
narratives, such as the exodus itself, but overwhelm-
ingly figurative and symbolic in prophetic and apocalyptic texts (see Isa 13:10-13; 34:4; Ezek 32:6-8; Hab
3:6-11).

4. The connections with the exodus plagues (hail and
fire, water to blood, darkness, locusts) draw our
attention to that ancient story of judgment and liberation. By thinking of the original exodus event, we
are reminded that God's judgments in history have a
liberative purpose; they are not arbitrary but have
a clear goal to bring liberation to humanity through
the punishment of evil and judgment of oppressors.

So clearly, the trumpets do not directly copy the seals. The different details instead function to provide a unique and important
perspective on the same period of time. We could spend a lot more

time focusing on the details, but that would defeat the purpose of this book to provide a brief overview and hopefully motivate you to further study. The recommended resources at the end of the book will provide further information on the details.

THE SEVEN THUNDERS

The visions that fill the interlude in Revelation 10–11 between the sixth and seventh trumpets function in a similar way to the visions in the interlude between the sixth and seventh seals in Revelation 7. These visions, which pause the narrative and delay the seventh seal and seventh trumpet, help us understand important details about the period between Jesus's first and second comings.

Revelation 10 first alerts us to the fact that there was originally another series of seven judgments, the seven thunders. John does not provide any details on the content of these judgments, but they provide an important parallel with the judgments described in Leviticus 26. In Leviticus 26:14–33, God describes four series of increasingly severe sevenfold punishments that were intended to lead his people to repentance if they began to compromise with idolatry and disobedience. This is similar to John's four series of seven punishments. Recognizing this parallel with Leviticus 26 helps us see that God's punishments are not primarily punitive but are intended to lead to repentance and restoration. At any point, someone can escape them through repentance. There is still time to set things right with God through repentance.

JOHN'S RECOMMISSIONING

John then recounts how he is recommissioned to prophesy (Rev 10:8–11). Like Ezekiel, he is told to eat a scroll representing the message of his prophecy (Ezek 2:8–3:3). The scroll is likely sweet because it reflects God's message but bitter because it involves judgment. This brief scene reminds us of the source of John's prophecy; he is communicating God's message.

THE TEMPLE

John then receives a short vision of the temple of God. He is told to "measure the temple of God and the altar and those who worship there" (Rev 11:1). In contrast, he is told not to measure the outer court of the temple because the holy city would be trampled for forty-two months.

This is sometimes interpreted to mean that there will someday be a literal rebuilt temple in Jerusalem, but such an interpretation is unlikely. For starters, the book of Hebrews makes it clear that Christ's once-and-for-all sacrifice fulfilled and set aside the sacrificial system forever (Heb 10:1–12). The vision in Revelation says nothing about the rebuilding of a literal temple, and John never refers to a literal earthly temple in Revelation. John's first hearers more likely would have thought about how the temple was often discussed by Christians in the broader Greco-Roman world. Both Peter and Paul give us insight into the significance of temple language when they describe God's people, both individually and together as communities, as God's temple, the place where God dwells through his Spirit (1 Cor 3:16–17; 6:19; 2 Cor 6:16; Eph 2:20–22; 1 Pet 2:4–10). This demonstrates that several decades before John wrote, the significance and meaning of the temple as God's dwelling place on earth had, for Christians (both Jew and gentile) who lived far from Jerusalem, shifted from the literal physical temple to the physical bodies of God's people.

The act of measuring likely represents protection in a way similar to God's seal. What is the significance of the protection of the inner court and trampling of the outer court, and why forty-two months? The answers to both of these questions become clearer when we read this vision in light of the closely connected vision of two witnesses.

THE TWO WITNESSES

The command to measure the temple morphs into a vision of two witnesses who prophesy for 1,260 days. This period of time matches the forty-two months during which the outer court of the temple would be trampled, so it is likely that these are parallel and not chronologically sequential visions.

Many interpreters throughout history have speculated about the identity of the two witnesses, and various suggestions have been given. Several clues suggest they are not specific individuals at all but rather represent all of God's people between Jesus's first and second comings. They are described as two lampstands (Rev 11:4), and John had earlier explicitly identified the lampstands as the churches (1:20). The number two likely reflects the need for every matter to be established by two witnesses (Deut 19:15). They are also identified as the two olive trees. This description links back to how Zechariah described the kingly and priestly figures (Zerubbabel and Joshua) as two olive trees (Zech 3:1–4:14). This is relevant because God's people are elsewhere described in Revelation as a kingdom of priests (Rev 1:6; 5:10). The biggest clue, however, that these two witnesses represent all of God's people between Jesus's first and second comings is the length of time. This three-and-a-half-year period was discussed already in part 1 above when illustrating principle 3 (recognize repetition), but it is worth reviewing briefly.

This three-and-a-half-year period of time is used to describe the trampling of the outer court (Rev 11:2), the time of the two witnesses (11:3), the time the woman is protected in the wilderness (12:6, 14), and the time that the beast has authority to persecute and kill God's people (13:5). There are many parallels among the visions that cover three and a half years. They all seem to end at the end, but only Revelation 12:5–6 provides a clear indication of when they begin. The three-and-a-half-year period begins with Jesus's resurrection and enthronement at God's right hand (12:5–6). This suggests that each of these visions of three-and-a-half years (the temple, the two witnesses, the woman in the wilderness, and the beast) describes this period from a different perspective and with different emphases. This is also the main period covered by the seven seals, trumpets, and bowls, so that most of the visions in Revelation cover the entire period between Jesus's first and second comings.

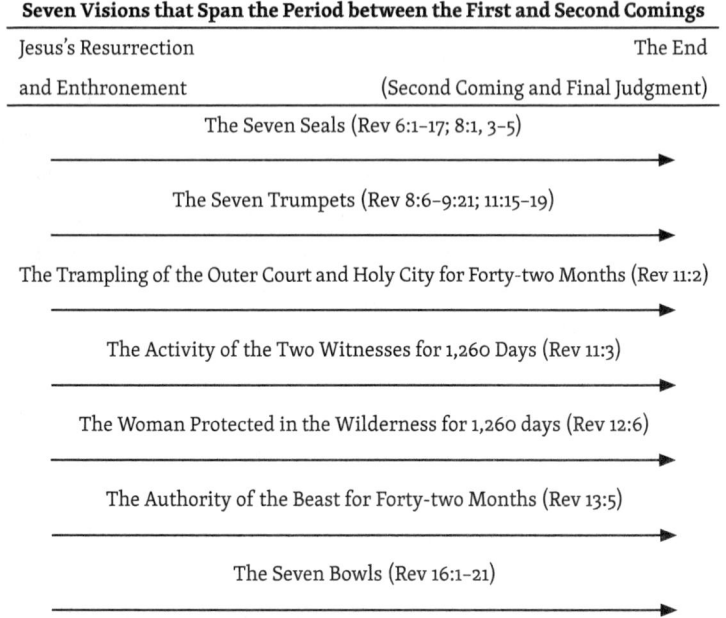

Seven Visions that Span the Period between the First and Second Comings

Jesus's Resurrection   The End
and Enthronement   (Second Coming and Final Judgment)

The Seven Seals (Rev 6:1–17; 8:1, 3–5)

The Seven Trumpets (Rev 8:6–9:21; 11:15–19)

The Trampling of the Outer Court and Holy City for Forty-two Months (Rev 11:2)

The Activity of the Two Witnesses for 1,260 Days (Rev 11:3)

The Woman Protected in the Wilderness for 1,260 days (Rev 12:6)

The Authority of the Beast for Forty-two Months (Rev 13:5)

The Seven Bowls (Rev 16:1–21)

Recognizing the two witnesses as representing God's people between Jesus's first and second comings helps us also recognize the vision of the temple as indicating the same thing. Both visions communicate the supernatural protection of God's people alongside the fact that they will be physically harmed. This also seems to be the main point of God's seal in Revelation 7 and the vision of the woman in the wilderness in chapter 12. These parallels suggest a common message throughout many of John's visions: *God's people are divinely protected in the present time for the purpose of witness, which will result in their persecution and eventual vindication.* Divine protection ensures that they are secure and will not experience God's wrath, but they are physically vulnerable and will experience opposition, persecution, and likely even death for their faith.

The two witnesses are described as protected by God; supernatural fire proceeds out of their mouths to destroy their opposers. This detail is best understood through a parallel in the book of Jeremiah, where God tells him, "Because you have spoken this word, behold, I am making my words in your mouth a fire … and the fire shall consume them" (Jer 5:14). God's message through Jeremiah is described as a fire that consumes the hearers. God's witnesses are also described as doing miracles similar to Elijah and Moses. This stresses the supernatural power that accompanies the activity of God's people through history.

God's People as Spiritually Protected	God's People as Physically Vulnerable
God's people are sealed (Rev 7:1–8).	They were killed (Rev 6:9–11).
The inner court of the temple is measured (Rev 11:1).	The outer court is trampled (Rev 11:2).
The two witnesses are protected (Rev 11:5).	The two witnesses are killed (Rev 11:7).
The woman is safe in the wilderness (Rev 12:13–16).	The woman's children are harmed (Rev 12:17).
Names are in the book of life (Rev 13:8).	They are taken captive and killed (Rev 13:10, 15).

The reference to the beast overcoming and killing them briefly previews the longer vision of the beast overcoming God's people in Revelation 13. Likewise, the account of their resurrection and ascension briefly points forward to resurrection and vindication in the visions of 20–22. Even though God's enemies reject and oppose God's faithful people, his people will be ultimately victorious. This victory will only come on the other side of suffering, death, and public humiliation (the refusal to bury the bodies).

The ending of the vision of the two witnesses describes the judgment of a tenth of humanity. The judgment motivates the rest of humanity to fear God and give him glory (Rev 11:13). This closely matches the "eternal gospel" that is announced to the world in chapter 14: "Fear God and give him glory, because the hour of his judgment has come, and worship him who made heaven and earth, the sea and the springs of water" (14:7). This suggests that the human beings who experience the witness of God's people and who survive God's judgment respond to the Gospel with fear and worship. It is not clear that this is a saving response, but it seems to imply such. It is a positive response to the message of God's witnesses combined with God's judgment.

Most of the visions in Revelation seem pessimistic about the fate of unbelieving humanity, and God's people are generally presented as an oppressed minority. For example, the sixth trumpet ends with a statement that "the rest of mankind, who were not killed by these plagues, did not repent of the works of their hands" (9:20). The positive ending to the vision of the two witnesses suggests that the witness of God's people plus judgment will effectively lead unbelievers to salvation in a way that judgment alone is not capable of doing.

This response of fearful worship helps us see that although the visions in Revelation describe how most people are deceived and worship the beast (see Rev 13), all hope is not lost. As God's people faithfully bear witness to the truth in the face of opposition, some, if not many, people will respond. The vision of the two witnesses is thus quite hopeful and anticipates earlier and later indications that many people will come to faith: the multitude of saved people in 7:9 was uncountable, the nations will walk by the light of the New Jerusalem (21:24), and the leaves of the tree of life are for the healing of the nations (22:2). Revelation certainly does not hold to universalism (the idea that all human beings will be saved in the end), but it is more optimistic than many people think. Humanity is caught in the middle. We are being actively deceived and misled while also receiving the witness of God's people to the truth of God, his salvation, and his judgment. Judgment will come against evil people who reject God, but there is still time and hope for repentance and faith.

THE SEVENTH TRUMPET

Recall that the mighty angel John saw in his vision in Revelation 10 swore an oath that "there would be no more delay" (10:6). This emphatic declaration leaves no doubt that the seventh trumpet represents the end. This oath is fulfilled when the seventh angel sounds the trumpet later (11:15). John doesn't narrate any events associated with the seventh trumpet but describes what happens through the use of hymns. With the seventh trumpet, "the kingdom of the world has become the kingdom of our Lord and of his Christ" (11:15). There will be no more interruptions or delays because "he shall reign forever and ever" (11:15). God is celebrated as the one "who is and who was" (11:17). He is no longer described as "the one who is to come" because with the seventh trumpet, he has come to his creation. The seventh trumpet is also "the time for the dead to be judged," the time "for rewarding your servants," and the time for "destroying the destroyers of the earth" (11:18). This is clearly the end, the coming of God and his Messiah, the final judgment, and the establishment of God's eternal kingdom on earth (not just the temporary millennial kingdom). The seventh trumpet, like the seventh seal, concludes with "flashes of lightning, rumblings, peals of thunder, an earthquake, and heavy hail" (11:19).

Like the description of the day of the Lord in the sixth and seventh seals, the seventh trumpet brings us to the end of history and the beginning of God's new creation. This means that later visions in Revelation 12–20 must go back in time from this moment to further describe events in history leading up to this point. This is exactly what we will find when we turn to Revelation 12 in the next chapter.

CONCLUSION

The seven trumpet judgments give us a different perspective and different details on the period between Jesus's first and second comings. Similar to the seven seals, the seven trumpets conclude at the final judgment. The fifth and sixth trumpets, in particular, assure us that God's people will not be subject to his wrath and are protected from demonic assault. The visions of the temple and two witnesses between the sixth and seventh trumpets help us as Christians to understand our identity and purpose during this same period of time. We are witnesses who will be spiritually protected while also being physically vulnerable.

This spiritual protection mixed with physical vulnerability explains the fact that even as we suffer along with the rest of humanity, we live with incredible confidence in God's presence, protection, and provision. We live with a confidence that from a purely human perspective could be viewed as naïve or silly, but our faith in God transforms our lives and gives us a hope and peace that this world cannot give nor take away. The seven trumpets communicate what the outcome of the present conflict on earth will be. Our Lord will reign fully, completely, and uncontested. This provides comfort and hope as well as motivation to repent and avoid compromise with the surrounding seductions of the world. We may feel like we are losing many battles, but we live with confidence that God will win the war, and our faithfulness to him is the most important thing in our lives.

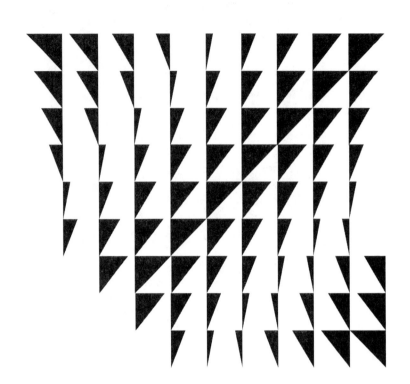

CHAPTER 11

The Dragon and Beasts

The seventh trumpet of Revelation 11 brought us to the end. God has come to his creation and established the eternal kingdom of his son. God has judged the dead, rewarded his people, and destroyed evil from his creation. The visions shared in Revelation 12–14 bring us back in time. They start before Jesus's birth, show the results of Jesus's death and resurrection, describe history as a time of conflict, and conclude, at the end of Revelation 14, with the final judgment. Even though this series of visions covers the same time period as the seals, trumpets, and two witnesses, it provides a unique perspective and new details. These visions focus on the spiritual warfare behind the persecution of God's people throughout history. The visions also make it clear that Satan and his allies can only persecute and kill God's people within a set period of time; God, not the devil, is in control of history. Finally, the visions raise the stakes by demonstrating that idolatry and compromise with the world are not innocent or accidental but involve rejection of God and allegiance to the devil himself. The picture is not all gloomy and depressing, however, because the visions also highlight God's initial victory over evil through Jesus's death and resurrection, as well as the final defeat of evil at the end of time. Evil exists on borrowed time, and its line of credit will not last forever.

Seeing the Big Picture

- The vision of the woman and the dragon in Revelation 12 describes the impact of Jesus's victory on the cross in the spiritual realm, shows that God's people are protected from spiritual harm, and reveals the malevolent spiritual power behind the persecution of Christians.

- The vision of the beasts in Revelation 13 shows how the dragon seeks to destroy God's people throughout history. Revelation 12–13 constitutes one continuous visionary narrative.

- Revelation 14 provides encouragement to God's people to persevere and gain victory over the dragon and beasts. John also sees a vision of two harvests, which contrasts ultimate salvation for God's people with judgment of those who worship the beast.

THE WOMAN AND THE DRAGON (REVELATION 12)

Three clear symbols anchor the interpretation of Revelation 12. First, Jesus is the male child who is brought to heaven to share God's throne. The child is identified as the Messiah by the reference to ruling the nations with a rod of iron, a description drawn from a messianic psalm (Ps 2:7–9). Second, Satan is the dragon, described as the serpent of Genesis 3:14–15. The dragon is presented as the leader of other fallen angels. John is looking back to Genesis with the shared motifs of woman, seed, serpent, and conflict. Third, the other children of the woman are Christians (both Jewish and gentile believers). The description of "those who keep the commandments of God and hold to the testimony of Jesus" (Rev 12:17) are two characteristic ways God's people are described throughout Revelation.

Based on these three foundational symbols, we can confidently understand the other images. The woman is not Mary but an overarching symbol for God's people. This matches the later description of God's people as the Lamb's bride (19:6–9; 21:9) and the contrast between the Lamb's bride and the prostitute Babylon (17–19). The symbol of the woman stresses continuity between the people of God both before and after Jesus was born. The spiritual dimension of the woman in Revelation 12 is emphasized by her heavenly clothing (the sun), and the crown of twelve stars likely links her to the twelve tribes of Israel.

The woman suffers intensely during the period of her pregnancy. This describes the suffering of God's people in the Old Testament and between the end of the Old Testament and the birth of Jesus. The dragon is pictured as waiting to devour the male child as soon as he is born (12:4). (I would love someday to see an apocalyptic Christmas card based on John's vision. Instead of an idyllic scene of shepherds and wise men at the stable, there would be a great seven-headed red dragon waiting to devour sweet baby Jesus as soon as he is laid in the manger.)

The dragon, of course, fails, and John's vision moves quickly from Jesus's birth to his ascension and enthronement. The woman, God's people, is then described as being protected and nourished for 1,260 days. There is no indication of a gap between Jesus's ascension and the beginning of this period; the 1,260 days (three-and-a-half years) begin at that point. This is the key to knowing when the visions of the temple, the two witnesses, and the two beasts begin because they are all described as covering this same period of time.

John's vision then shifts to show the impact of Jesus's enthronement in the heavenly realms. Because of Jesus's death, resurrection, and enthronement, the dragon is cast out of heaven to earth. This means not that he becomes physical and material but that he is cast from a higher spiritual realm to the lowest spiritual realm that exists parallel to the created material world. This casting down of Satan is interpreted as ending his ability to accuse God's people. Because of Jesus's death, he is no longer able to bring accusations against those whom God has declared not guilty. This theological interpretation of Satan's defeat parallels Paul's celebration in Romans 8:33–34: "Who shall bring any charge against God's elect? It is God who justifies. Who is to condemn? Christ Jesus is the one who died—more than that, who was raised—who is at the right hand of God, who indeed is interceding for us." John's apocalyptic vision of the casting down of the great accuser makes the same point as Paul's more theological discussion. The participation of God's people in the victory over the dragon is attributed to the blood of the Lamb (Jesus's sacrificial death) and to the faith expressed in their witness/ testimony to the point of death (Rev 12:11).

Jesus's victory through resurrection and enthronement is presented as the decisive victory over Satan, but it is not the final victory. The most crucial battle has been won, but there are still more battles to be fought. Satan has no ability to undermine God's people in the divine council in heaven, but he can still seek to destroy them on earth. John's vision next describes the dragon as filled with wrath and seeking to destroy the woman. He knows that his time is short, that is, limited. He is defeated in his attempt to destroy the woman; she is supernaturally protected, and he cannot touch her (12:13–16). Revelation 12 ends with a change of strategy. He cannot spiritually harm God's people, but he can physically harm them. This is described as his war against the rest of her offspring (12:17). God's people are spiritually protected and untouchable, but they can be harmed physically.

THE TWO BEASTS (REVELATION 13)

Revelation 12 ends with the dragon standing on the edge of the sea, and Revelation 13 begins with a beast rising from the sea. It is as if the dragon has summoned or recruited an ally in his mission to make war on the children of the woman. The dragon empowers the beast with all of its own power to carry on its lethal mission (13:2).

In the discussion of principle 2 (let the original historical context guide your interpretation), we considered how the first readers would have easily recognized the first beast as the Roman empire and the second beast as the local provincial government in Asia Minor. We looked at an example from Pliny the Younger of how the local rulers persecuted Christians and required them to worship the image of the emperor to save their lives and avoid persecution. Emperor worship and local persecution provide the main background for understanding how the first hearers would have understood these visions. In this chapter, we won't repeat the evidence and arguments from chapter 2; instead, we'll comment on issues not discussed there.

There are indications that even though the first beast would have been understood as Rome by John and his first hearers, it was also intended to be trans-temporal, to span the whole period of time between Jesus's first and second comings. This is evident from the forty-two-month time period that matches the same period in the other visions. It is also evident from the way the beast in Revelation 13 draws characteristics from all four of Daniel's beasts (Dan 7:3–8). Daniel's four beasts represent four nations that span hundreds of years. John's beast thus likely represents many nations over long periods of time. The first readers would have identified the beast with the idolatry and oppression of Rome, but many nations throughout history fit the bill to various degrees. Power tends to corrupt, and powerful nations are easily manipulated by Satan to either actively oppress God's faithful people or seek to deceive and lure them into compromise with idolatry through promises of wealth and security.

The reference to the beast having a mortal wound that was healed points to a theme of satanic imitation of divine reality. This imitation is aimed at counterfeiting truth in order to deceive. The second beast had "two horns like a lamb" (13:11), but it certainly wasn't a lamb. Just as Jesus was slain and conquered death, one of the heads of the beast appeared to be slain and healed. The first readers likely would have thought of the devastating events of AD 69, during which many people thought the Roman Empire was at its end. With Vespasian's rule, however, the empire recovered completely. This historical explanation is possible, but the detail that the beast was wounded and healed could also make a theological point. The beast was decisively defeated by Jesus on the cross, but evil still exists in the world and seems to be completely recovered. The survival of evil for a time, even after Jesus's enthronement, could suggest that the beast is the one with real authority and power. It appears unstoppable. The whole earth buys into the lie and asks, "Who is like the beast, and who can fight against it?" (Rev 13:4). This is a powerful question, and John's visions do not immediately answer it. The answer comes in the vision of the Lamb's victory over the beast in 17:13–14.

The beast is given incredible authority (13:5–8). It seems to have free reign to make war on God's people and conquer them and to rule over "every tribe and people and language and nation" (13:7). God's people, however, exist as a powerful insurgency and resistance movement from "every tribe and language and people and nation" (5:9; 7:9).

God's people are assured of ultimate victory because their names are written in the Lamb's book of life (13:8), but they are also informed that they would experience captivity and slaughter because of the onslaught of the beast (13:10). John's vision certainly does not promise Christians their best life now. But John does not want this vision to lead to despair and indicates the purpose he hopes it will have: "Here is a call for the endurance and faith of the saints" (13:10). We do not give up because the power of the beast seems unstoppable; we endure because we know the final outcome. We know that we are called to overcome in the same way that the slain Lamb overcame—by faithfulness to the point of death. We must be faithful even when evil seems to triumph.

Just as the dragon recruited the first beast to carry out his war against God's people, the first beast recruits a second beast to enforce its rule. This second beast is empowered to perform miracles as a form of demonic deception (13:13–15). There are accounts from antiquity of tricks used to fool people into believing that an idol was able to move or speak along with artificial manipulation of lighting and sounds. John's visions could refer to tricks that convince people that the beasts have supernatural power, or they could refer to the genuine expression of demonic spiritual power in imitation of God's power.

The second beast enforces worship of the first beast and requires everyone to receive a mark on the right hand or the forehead (13:16). The mark is associated with the name of the beast, and those who refuse the mark are unable to participate in the world economically (13:17). This economic exclusion likely further describes how those who do not worship the beast are killed (13:15).

The beast's mark is just another instance of counterfeiting. All of God's people have his seal, identified as his name, on their foreheads to mark ownership and allegiance. God's seal rests on those who worship him. The beast's mark on the forehead or hand likewise signifies ownership and allegiance and rests on those who worship the beast. The location of the mark on the forehead imitates the location of God's seal, but the mention of a mark on the hand likely strengthens the connection with buying and selling. Imperial Roman coins had the image of the emperor on the front surrounded by inscriptions that were likely viewed by Jews and Christians as blasphemous (Emperor, divine Augustus, greatest priest, father of the country, etc.). The backs of imperial coins normally featured an idolatrous deity with other, often blasphemous, inscriptions. The usage of idolatrous coins could be seen as identification with the idolatrous imperial and economic system. The connection of emperor worship with imperial coins also helps explain the detail of the beast's heads covered with blasphemous names (13:1) and the beast's "mouth uttering haughty and blasphemous words" (13:5). If the connection of the mark of the beast to coins is on track, it suggests that John's visions anticipate a future in which faithfulness to Jesus would involve complete exclusion from normal economic life (although there were various provincial coins that were less associated with emperor worship).

Every mention of the mark of the beast in Revelation is connected to worship of the beast (13:16, 17; 14:9, 11; 16:2; 19:20; 20:4). John never mentions the mark without reference to idolatrous worship. This recognition will help us avoid some unlikely interpretations. It seems common in some circles for Christians to think of the mark of the beast as a computer chip implanted in people. The chip will theoretically help prevent identity fraud and function as a bank card and electronic key. Instead of paying with cash, you will someday just be able to scan your hand at the checkout. The first problem with this interpretation relates to principle 2 (let the original historical context guide your interpretation). If the proposed interpretation would have made no sense to the original hearers, it should automatically be viewed as unlikely. This does not mean the interpretation is impossible, but it should be our last resort. The connection of the mark to allegiance and worship also makes the computer chip interpretation unlikely. Nobody will be judged by God simply for getting a computer chip implanted on their body. This may be an ill-advised thing to do based on privacy concerns in light of Big Brother, but it is not the mark of the beast unless it is connected to allegiance and worship. No Christian will ever end up saying, "I thought this computer chip would help protect my identity and keep me from ever losing my keys and wallet again, but now I am damned for eternity!" *The mark is always connected to allegiance and worship.*

This observation leads to the most likely interpretation. It is clear from Revelation 22:4 that all of God's people will have his name on their foreheads. The vision also suggests that all the rest of humanity receive the mark of the beast (13:16). The point seems clear: every human being will be sealed or marked; there is no neutral third party. You will have either God's seal or the beast's mark of ownership. All of humanity is divided into one camp or the other. Few, if any, interpreters argue that God's seal can be visibly and physically seen by human eyes, and it is likely similar with the beast's mark. Those with the beast's mark declare allegiance to the beast and enjoy economic success and security in this present time, while those with God's seal bear witness to God's rule and experience persecution, marginalization, suffering, and death in the present time. Revelation 13 ends on this dismal note, but Revelation 14 reveals the great reversal that will take place in the future.

Even though John's visions describe all of humanity as being in two camps, the line between them is porous, not firm. We saw in the proclamations to the seven churches that it was possible for Christians to have their lampstands removed (2:5), to have their names blotted from the book of life (3:5), or to be spit out of Jesus's mouth (3:16). Christians must persevere in faithfulness to prevent compromise and sharing in God's punishment of the wicked (18:4). Conversely, it is also evident that non-Christians are invited to repent and switch allegiances (22:17). The strict division of humanity into two camps is not deterministic but motivational. This division confronts us with the reality that there are ultimately only two options and calls on us to overcome through repentance, worship, witness, obedience, and perseverance.

Finally, how should we understand the number of the beast, 666? The text is pretty clear here: the number corresponds to a name. Since numbers in antiquity were expressed by letters, it was common practice to calculate the number of someone's name. *Alpha* represents 1, *beta* represents 2, *gamma* represents 3, *delta* represents 4, etc. This can be done in Greek or Hebrew. Many interpreters observe that it is easy to determine a number when you know the name but very difficult to determine the name when you only know the number. Many names have been proposed throughout history, but the most likely option comes from the way that "Nero Caesar" equals 666 when transliterated from Greek into Hebrew. This seems to make sense of the way that the mark of the beast is 616 in some ancient manuscripts of Revelation; 616 is the result of transliterating "Nero Caesar" from Latin (instead of Greek) into Hebrew.[1] It seems evident that some, if not many, early Christians viewed the number as a reference to Nero, although Nero likely died decades before John wrote Revelation. This could

---

1. For a more detailed discussion of the connection of letters and numbers in antiquity, see David E. Aune, *Revelation 6-16*, Word Biblical Commentary 52B (Nashville: Thomas Nelson, 1998), 770-773.

be explained by the fact that many people believed that Nero, similar to Elvis, was not really dead and, unlike Elvis, would return to wage war against Rome at the head of an army from Parthia, Rome's main rival in the East in the first century. More likely, Nero is the answer because he was the most infamous tyrant and persecutor of Christians in the first century. He is traditionally associated with the execution of both Peter and Paul in Rome, and he brutally killed many Christians after blaming them for causing a devasting fire in Rome. Nero was thus the symbolic and typological figurehead for the dragon's use of the beast to wage war against the children of the woman. Future persecutors are simply following Nero's lead.

To the extent to which global leaders are used by the dragon to further its war against God's people and oppress humanity, we can see them as connected to the trans-temporal beast, but it is well past time for Christians to stop trying to connect different contemporary leaders with *the* beast. Hitler was not *the* beast, although he certainly functioned as an expression of the beast in his generation. The leader of Russia is not the beast. The president of the US is not the beast (even if he's not from your preferred political party). No individual in the future is the beast, although many leaders in the past, present, and future represent the beast and seek to fulfill the dragon's purposes in various ways at various times. This is similar to what John teaches Christians about the antichrist elsewhere: there are lots of antichrists, and they are already here (1 John 2:18, 22; 4:3; 2 John 7). Revelation never discusses the antichrist per se, but the beast functions in a similar way. The beast represents governments and world leaders who oppose God's purposes and people from the first century until the second coming of Christ.

MOTIVATIONAL VISIONS (REVELATION 14:1—13)

Revelation 13 ends on a dark note, but the first vision of chapter 14 shows us God's people in victory and at rest. They are standing in victory with the Lamb on Mount Zion, a reference forward to the New Jerusalem, which descends to earth in chapter 21. The vision of believers in victory, like parallel visions throughout Revelation, blurs the line between the intermediate state and resurrection life in God's new creation by using imagery associated with both. The image of God's people as an army being counted and prepared for holy war in 7:5–8 is continued here, but now they are shown as victorious and not just as preparing for battle.

They are described as redeemed and blameless male virgins who follow the Lamb wherever he goes. The idea that they are virgins should not be understood to exclude married Christians but rather connects with how God's people are described as the Lamb's bride later in the book (19:6–8). They have resisted the sexual immorality connected with idolatry, against which several of the seven proclamations in Revelation 2–3 warn. Some interpreters connect this virginity with how Israel's soldiers in the Old Testament were supposed to abstain from sexual activity to maintain ceremonial purity before armed conflict (1 Sam 21:5). This interpretation explains why they are described as male and fits with the theme of God's people engaged in a holy war through their witness. The symbolism, however, does not literalistically exclude women (note the later feminine imagery of the Lamb's bride), and the virgin status highlights their avoidance of idolatry, which is closely connected with sexual immorality in Revelation and in the Old Testament prophets.

This vision shows the end result of those who are killed for refusing the beast's mark at the end of Revelation 13. They refuse to worship and serve the beast and are killed. They overcome the beast by being overcome by the beast. They suffer for not having the beast's mark, but now they are shown as celebrating and victorious, with the Lamb's name and the Father's name written on their foreheads. It seems that there is only enough room on one's forehead to declare allegiance to one side or the other; no one can serve two masters.

This vision of God's people in victory is followed by a vision of three angels who each make a proclamation. The first angel proclaims the eternal gospel: "Fear God and give him glory" (14:7). This proclamation functions to call all of humanity to worship God. Although every person must take sides, and there is no third option, their fate is not determined in advance, and "every nation and tribe and language and people" is presented with the gospel and called on to make the right choice (14:6).

The second angel announces the fall of Babylon the Great. This is the first reference to Babylon the Great in Revelation, but she will be the central focus of future visions. For now, we are alerted to the fact that she has been judged because she "made all the nations drink the wine of the passion of her sexual immorality" (14:8).

The third angel follows with a strong warning directed toward those who worship the beast and its image and receive its mark. Such people will experience God's wrath in a public forum, and the smoke of their torment will go up forever. The public nature of the punishment ("in the presence of the holy angels and in the presence of the Lamb") intensifies the horror of the punishment in a culture oriented toward issues of honor and shame. The smoke ascending forever and ever and the lack of rest day or night suggest eternal conscious punishment. This third angelic proclamation stresses the fact that the easy road in life (avoidance of persecution through compromise with the beast) leads to an eternal lack of rest. The next verse presents the opposite side of the picture: those who die in the Lord will have rest (14:13).

In 14:12, John summarizes the main point of the visions in 12–14. Knowledge of the eternal results of our current choices calls "for the endurance of the saints." John shares these visions with us not to satisfy our curiosity about the future but to issue an urgent call for us to persevere in faithfulness to God no matter the cost. John is not like a prosperity gospel preacher or a salesman who deceitfully minimizes the cost in order to get people to follow. Instead, like Jesus, who focused on the need for his disciples to take up their crosses daily, he focuses on the costs involved. He does not minimize how terrible things might get in this present life but highlights the potential horror that those who resist the beast will likely experience. He also stresses that the end result will be worth any cost.

TWO HARVESTS (REVELATION 14:14—20)

The end result of the two possible courses of life (allegiance to the beast or allegiance to the Lamb) is further emphasized by the concluding visions of Revelation 14. John first sees a grain harvest in which the Son of Man harvests the earth. Throughout Scripture, grain harvests are normally positive events. Grape harvests, on the other hand, are more often connected with God's judgment due to the imagery surrounding the trampling of grapes in a winepress. The first harvest thus suggests God's protection and salvation of his people; they experienced the wrath of the dragon, but they will not experience God's wrath. The second harvest, on the other hand, describes God's punishment of the wicked.

The fuller description of Jesus's return, the last battle, and judgment in Revelation 19:11-21 parallels this description of a grape harvest.

Rev 14:19-20	Rev 19:15
So the angel swung his sickle across the earth and gathered the grape harvest of the earth and threw it into *the great winepress of the wrath of God. And the winepress was trodden outside the city*, and blood flowed from the winepress, as high as a horse's bridle, for 1,600 stadia.	From his mouth comes a sharp sword with which to strike down the nations, and he will rule them with a rod of iron. He will *tread the winepress of the fury of the wrath of God* the Almighty.

The similar imagery of tramping the winepress of God's wrath indicates that these visions are describing the same final events. Revelation 14, like most of the main visions in Revelation, brings us right up to the end.

CONCLUSION

Similar to other visions, the series of visions in Revelation 12–14 begins with Jesus's enthronement and ends at the end, the second coming and final judgment. Again, Revelation's parallel visions do not simply repeat themselves; each visionary retelling of the course of history provides unique details and perspectives. The visions in Revelation 12–14 are at the book's heart, and they expose the true source of evil and persecution in the world. The dragon is full of wrath and has recruited two beasts to help him wage a war against Christians. This war is fought through both outward persecution and more subtle deception and temptation to compromise to avoid persecution and gain economic security and benefit. These are the same themes that were stressed in the seven proclamations to the churches (Rev 2–3).

In addition to exposing the source of opposition to God and his people, these visions stress the suffering and persecution that God's people are likely to experience in life if they are faithful to God. Revelation 13, by itself, would function as a good promotional advertisement for the beast; it provides compelling reasons for Christians to compromise. The visions of Revelation 14, however, complete the picture and show the end results of one's allegiance in life.

These chapters also teach us who we are and what we need to do. We are God's people who must bear faithful witness unto death. We will be persecuted, but we are promised God's supernatural spiritual protection. The dragon has already been defeated in heaven and has but a limited time to wage war against us. Our victory is sure!

CHAPTER 12

The Seven Bowls

J ohn indicates that the seven bowl judgments are the last because they complete the wrath of God. "Then I saw another sign in heaven, great and amazing, seven angels with seven plagues, which are the last, for with them the wrath of God is finished" (Rev 15:1). The seven bowl visions are not the last visions that John receives since we are not at the end of the book. This statement of finality, however, stresses that the seven bowl judgments bring us right up to the end, the final battle and last judgment. The seventh bowl describes the end of God's judgment and wrath (15:5-8). The later visions in Revelation 17-20 zoom in and give different perspectives and details regarding the last battle that is described in the sixth and seventh bowls.

THE SONG OF MOSES AND THE LAMB

After introducing the seven angels with the seven last plagues in 15:1, John concludes the visions of the dragon-beast cycle (12-14) by showing God's people in victory and celebration. By being conquered by the beast, they "had conquered the beast and its image and the number of its name" (15:2). They are pictured as singing a song of worship, "the song of Moses, the servant of God, and the song of the Lamb" (15:3). This connection with Moses reminds us again of the original exodus, the foundational historical example of God saving his people through the judgment of evil oppressors. This prepares us for the bowl judgments, which are closely modeled after the exodus judgments. The judgments have a redemptive goal and lead to a new exodus, the final liberation and salvation of God's people.

Seeing the Big Picture

The seven bowls further describe God's judgment of the world. They conclude with the final battle and highlight the theme of God's justice.

The content of the song stresses the justice of God's actions and offers a hopeful vision of the future. God's justice is highlighted by the declarations "just and true are your ways" and "your righteous acts have been revealed" (15:3-4). Some people become uncomfortable when thinking about God's judgment and punishment. It is not fun to think about punishment because it is so common for punishment to be abusive or unjust in this broken world. Those in power abuse their power and oppress those who are too weak to defend themselves. God is unimaginably powerful and could use his power to oppress people in an arbitrary, random, mean, or unfair way. Who could stop him?

It is important for us to recognize that the problem is not with power per se but with the character and intentions of those in power. Those who are loving, good, and just exercise power with good motives, with wisdom, and in a way that brings beneficial results. Those who are wicked, cruel, arrogant, insecure, and greedy exercise power oppressively and destructively.

This hymn celebrates the fact that God's actions are true and just. We celebrate God's character because it is precisely his character that enables us to trust that he will do what's right. It is hard for human beings to think about punishment without thinking about abuse. We quickly visualize a drunk and angry father who lashes out at his employees, kicks his dog, and beats his wife and children for no reason at all. But God is not like that.

The hymn repeats the eternal gospel that was announced in 14:7: "Who will not fear, O Lord, and glorify your name?" (15:4). This is how those who experienced the witness of God's people and God's judgment responded at the end of Revelation 11. They feared God and gave him glory (11:13). Similarly, this hymn strikes a hopeful note: "All nations will come and worship you" (15:4). The seven bowl judgments portray a dismal picture of people refusing to repent, but this hymn alerts us to the fact that many people, indeed, from every nation, will reject worship of the beast and respond to God with true worship.

THE SEVEN BOWLS OF GOD'S WRATH

Unlike the seven seals and seven trumpets, there is no lengthy break between the sixth and seventh bowl judgments; they rush forward at almost breakneck speed. There are a few brief pauses, which are used to reflect on the justice of the judgments or on the refusal of those who oppose God to repent. The seven bowl judgments are modeled on the exodus plagues, and five have direct parallels with the trumpet judgments.

	Trumpets		Bowls
2nd	a third of the sea turned to blood and a third of the creatures in it die	2nd	sea turned to blood and all creatures in it die
3rd	a third of the fresh water is embittered	3rd	fresh water turned to blood
4th	a third of light darkened	5th	darkness on earth
6th	troops gathered at the Euphrates	6th	kings and armies come from across the Euphrates
7th	lightning, earthquake, hail	7th	lightning, earthquake, hail

The main difference lies in the intensification of the bowl judgments. They are not limited to one-third but are described as global and universal. Nobody can escape. This does not require a chronological progression in which the seven trumpets happen and then the seven bowls happen. Chronological progression is rendered unlikely because of how the sixth of both sequences seems to describe the same event (note the Euphrates), and it is rendered impossible because of how the seventh trumpet describes the final judgment. It is far more likely that the intensification in the narrative suggests that things will get worse as history progresses. This fits the metaphor of birth pains Jesus uses to describe the wars, famines, and natural disasters (earthquakes) that would take place throughout human history.

The Euphrates River is mentioned in both the sixth trumpet and the sixth bowl (9:14; 16:12). The Euphrates is one of the most significant rivers in that part of the world, and many Old Testament prophets highlight it (or invaders coming from the north) in their prophecies of God's judgment of his sinful people. In the first century, people would have thought of the Parthian empire beyond the Euphrates, but John's visions are not focused on the Parthians as the end-time adversaries.

When discussing the trumpets, I argued that the plagues were symbolic or figurative and should not be taken literally. A literal interpretation is unlikely for several reasons. The plagues of the sixth trumpet and the bowl judgments are threatened against people throughout history (Rev 22:18); they are not literally experienced only by people living at the end of time. How could the sun, moon and stars be darkened by a third if they have already been completely darkened in the sixth seal (6:12–13)? Why are the locusts of the fifth trumpet told not to harm the grass (9:4) after all the grass had been burned up in the first trumpet (8:7)? These inconsistencies evaporate when the judgments are understood symbolically. Apocalyptic visions are not concerned with logical consistency. This symbolic interpretation of the exodus plagues is confirmed by the sixth bowl when three demonic spirits like frogs come out of the mouths of the dragon, the beast, and the false prophet (16:13–14). The frog plague was literal in the original exodus narratives, but in Revelation these are not literal frogs.

Even though the seven bowl judgments largely overlap in meaning and in time with the seven seals and seven trumpets, they offer several unique perspectives and details. The seven seals suggest that God's judgments, at least in part, consist of God handing human beings over to our own devices. We harm ourselves through oppression, warfare, and civil unrest, which leads to famine and pandemics. The seven trumpets focus on how God does not protect unbelievers from demonic spiritual oppression; those who do not have his seal are oppressed, deceived, and killed by malicious demonic activity.

The seven bowls highlight both God's direct involvement in these judgments and the justice of God's actions. The bowls are explicitly described as the expression of God's wrath (15:1, 7; 16:1, 19). He brought the judgments (16:5) and had power over the plagues (16:9). God is explicitly presented as more active and involved than at any other point in the narrative.

Two statements interrupt the third and fourth bowl judgments to stress the justice of God's actions. First, an angel declares, "Just are you, O Holy One, who is and who was, for you brought these judgments. For they have shed the blood of saints and prophets, and you have given them blood to drink. It is what they deserve" (16:5–6). The blood of the saints and prophets draws our attention back to the souls under the altar crying out for justice in the fifth seal (6:9–11). This connection is confirmed by the next verse: "And I heard the altar saying, 'Yes, Lord God the Almighty, true and just are your judgments' " (16:7). It is not particularly unexpected to encounter a talking altar in the apocalyptic genre (see 9:13), but the connection of the altar with a celebration of justice explicitly connects back to the fifth seal. This connection highlights the justice of God's judgments as an answer to the prayer of his people for justice and vindication.

John inserts an important message from Jesus right into the middle of his discussion of the sixth bowl judgment. This is an unusual insertion and highlights principle 1 (focus on the original purpose of the visions). "Behold, I am coming like a thief! Blessed is the one who stays awake, keeping his garments on, that he may not go about naked and be seen exposed!" (16:15). The metaphor of a thief normally stresses the fact that we will not be able to know the timing; Jesus will return unexpectedly. Thieves do not come when you expect or want them to. Jesus's message highlights the symbolic nature of the judgments and the imminence of his return. If the judgments were literal, we would easily be able to calculate things. We could say, "Well, everyone was just scorched by a super-hot sun [the fourth bowl judgment], so now we need to prepare for darkness and painful sores [the fifth bowl judgment]." The judgments will not be quite so obvious, and Jesus could return at any point. Our inability to pinpoint the timing or to know whether he could come today or centuries from now has a motivational purpose: we must constantly be morally and spiritually ready and alert. This is the main focus of Jesus's teaching on his second coming in the Gospels. We must not allow ourselves to be lulled into spiritual sleep by the demonically inspired seductions of the surrounding world or to be cowed into complacency through fear of persecution.

Although the battle is not narrated, the sixth and seventh bowls set the stage for the final battle and hint at its conclusion. The battle is presented as a global gathering of the kings of the whole world for a confrontation at Armageddon. The battle is concluded with God's declaration, "It is done!" (16:17), flashes of lightning, rumblings, thunder, a severe earthquake, the removal of islands and mountains, and enormous hailstones (16:18–21).

The removal of islands and mountains matches the events associated with the day of the Lord in the sixth seal (6:14) and the cosmic upheaval of the great white throne judgment in chapter 20: "Then I saw a great white throne and him who was seated on it. From his presence earth and sky fled away, and no place as found for them" (20:11).

This final global battle also matches descriptions of the Gog-Magog episode from Ezekiel 38-39. Ezekiel's vision describes a deceptive gathering of global forces to fight against God's people (Ezek 38:2-7, 15). The battle in Ezekiel involves God's use of an earthquake, the demolishment of mountains, hail, and fiery brimstone (Ezek 38:19-22). Significantly, the location, Armageddon, also connects this battle to Ezekiel 38-39. Armageddon, despite what is commonly claimed, has nothing to do with the mountain of Megiddo because there is no such mountain. It instead relates to the Hebrew for "mountain of meeting/gathering" and is connected to Jerusalem, the location of the final cosmic battle involving both spiritual and physical beings in scriptural prophecy.[1]

Several of the upcoming visions in Revelation 17-20 also focus on this final battle scene, and we will discuss it in more detail in the following chapters. Despite multiple references to this final battle in Revelation, the actual conflict is never narrated; there are no clashing swords. God and Jesus put an end to the battle with their coming. It is not a literal battle, with millions of soldiers physically surrounding the city of Jerusalem in Israel, but rather, it reflects an intense and severe global persecution of Christians right before Jesus returns.

CONCLUSION

The seven bowl judgments closely parallel the seven seal and trumpet judgments in how they depict God's judgment of evil between Jesus's first and second comings. As we should now expect, they do not just copy the other series of judgments; they provide unique details and perspectives. First, the seven bowl judgments highlight

---

1. The detailed argumentation necessary for this point would bog the chapter down too much. If you are interested in exploring this further see Meredith G. Kline, "Har Magedon: The End of the Millennium," *JETS* 39 (1996): 207-222.

God's direct involvement in the punishment. Second, they underscore the justness and rightness of God's actions. Justice is being carried out! Third, the fact that Jesus's return will be like a thief motivates us to remain spiritually and morally alert and active. There will be multiple reasons to compromise or slowly slide into complacency, but we as Christians are called on to constantly encourage and help each other be ready for Jesus's return.

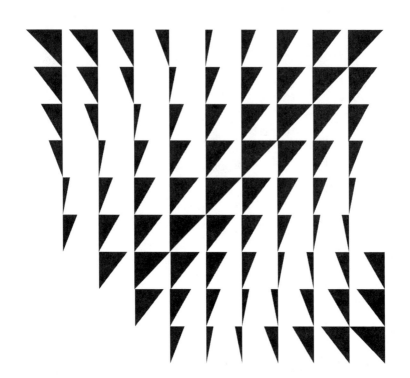

CHAPTER 13

Babylon the Great

Near the end of the seventh bowl judgment, John casually notes, "And God remembered Babylon the great, to make her drain the cup of the wine of the fury of his wrath" (Rev 16:19). This picks up on the brief announcement of the fall of Babylon the Great in 14:8, but who is she? What is her role? Why is she being punished? Up to this point, we do not know much about this character. That is about to change.

Revelation 17–18 focuses on Babylon the Great, her partnership with the beast, and her destruction. The judgments described in these chapters likely take place in history at the same time as the seventh bowl judgment, even though they are narrated after the fact. John's narrative strategy seems intentional. He introduces God's adversaries in a certain order and narrates their judgment in reverse order. For example, Death and Hades are introduced in chapters 1 and 6, the dragon comes in chapter 12, the beasts enter in 13 (apart from the brief preview in 11:7), and Babylon the Great appears in 14. John then narrates the judgment of the main foes in reverse order: Babylon the Great in 17-18, the beasts in 19, the dragon in 20:10, and Death and Hades in 20:14. The actual judgment of these adversaries likely takes place in a closely connected series of events, but each one is given its own moment to shine in the narrative of John's visions.

Seeing the Big Picture

• The great prostitute, Babylon the Great, is a complex image symbolizing the religious, economic, and cultural dimensions of the dragon's attempt to destroy God's people.

• Babylon the Great was identified as Rome in the first century, but it includes systems of temptation, corruption, exploitation, and oppression throughout history. She is seductive, powerful, and exploitative. She is allied with the political and military power of the beast to support the dragon's attempt to destroy God's people.

• God is capable of using evil forces to judge evil, and he directs the beast and its allies to destroy Babylon the Great. The Lamb will conquer the beast and its allies in a final battle, which corresponds to the battle described in the sixth and seventh bowl judgments.

• God's people are called to separate from Babylon's sins of idolatry, sexual immorality, and living in prideful luxury through the oppression and exploitation of others.

BABYLON THE GREAT

One of the seven angels connected to the seven bowls takes the lead to show John a new vision. John is told in advance what he is about to see: the judgment of the great prostitute with whom the kings of earth committed sexual immorality and who made all the inhabitants of the earth drunk with her sexual immorality (Rev 17:1–2). When John sees the prostitute, she is sitting on the beast with seven heads and ten horns from chapter 13.

The description of the prostitute gives us several clues to her identity. Just as God and the dragon are put in explicit opposition and the sea beast is described as a counterfeit of the Lamb, the land beast and the prostitute exist as counterparts to God's people (the Lamb's bride and the woman from chapter 12). This correspondence alerts us to the fact that just as the dragon and beasts are in conflict with God and the Lamb throughout the period between Jesus's first and second comings, the prostitute also exists throughout that time. She meets her end in the seventh bowl judgment at the end of the final battle and the return of Christ.

The first hearers would have immediately connected the prostitute with the city of Rome, the city that ruled the world. Babylon destroyed Jerusalem in the Old Testament, and Rome became a new Babylon by destroying Jerusalem in AD 70. Babylon thus became an easy code word for Rome. This connection is made explicit when the angel interprets the seven heads of the beast as the seven mountains on which the woman was seated (17:9). The image of the goddess Roma sitting on the seven hills of Rome was an easily recognizable symbol, and Rome was widely known as the city on seven hills. The angel tells John that "the woman that you saw is the great city that has dominion over the kings of the earth" (17:18). The prostitute thus has a widely recognized connection to the goddess Roma, the personified deification of Rome who was literally worshipped throughout the Empire. Thus, there is a *religious* dimension to the symbol of Babylon the Great.

She is much more complex than that, however. Her clothing matches many of the economic products described in Revelation 18: purple, scarlet, gold, jewels, and pearls (vv. 12, 16). Revelation 18:16 describes the city as wearing these products in the same way that John sees the prostitute wearing them: "Alas, alas, for the great city that was clothed in fine linen, in purple and scarlet, adorned with gold, with jewels, and with pearls!" The Lamb's bride is also clothed with fine linen (19:8). The bride's fine linen is interpreted as the righteous deeds of the saints, while the prostitute's fine linen is the result of exploitative and oppressive trade. There is a dimension of *economic exploitation* to the symbol of Babylon the Great. Immense wealth is centralized in one place; all those who participate with her are promised a share in her wealth.

She is still more complex than that. John sees that the woman was "drunk with the blood of the saints, the blood of the martyrs of Jesus" (17:6). There is a dimension of *religious persecution* to the symbol of Babylon the Great. Pulling all of this together, we can identify Babylon the Great as a complex image symbolizing the religious, economic, and cultural dimensions of opposition to God and his people. She is seductive, powerful, and exploitative. This contrasts with the beast, which is connected to political and military power. While the beast forces compliance through explicit persecution and murder, the prostitute seduces victims with promises of pleasure and wealth. Both enemies can be deadly for Christians.

THE BEAST

John's vision then switches to focus on the beast. Revelation 17:7–12 is the most difficult passage to interpret in the entire book, no matter what interpretive approach you take. The difficulty lies in how the meanings of the symbols are constantly in flux. It is said that the beast "is not" (vv. 8, 11), but one of the heads currently "is" (v. 10). The heads are seven mountains, but they are also seven kings (v. 9). The ten horns also happen to be ten kings (v. 12). It is also said that the beast itself is an eighth king (v. 11). It's easy to lose one's bearings in the midst of this interpretive and symbolic whirlwind.

One possible interpretive approach relates to the first readers: how would they have understood this? They would have been tempted to count Roman rulers; the one that "is" was the sixth head and the current emperor. The end could thus be expected to come two emperors after the current one. Readers at the end of the first century, however, would have recognized this approach as unlikely. If the sixth emperor were Domitian (AD 81–96), then the eighth would be Trajan, but that would make the first emperor to be Gaius (AD 37–41). Nobody in the ancient world would start an emperor list with Gaius. If the sixth emperor were Nero (AD 54–68), the first emperor would be Julius Caesar (49–44 BC), the proper first emperor, but the eighth emperor would be the short-lived and insignificant Otho (AD 69). No reader after AD 70 would have thought that Otho was the eighth, and John likely did not even write Revelation until the early-to-mid-90s.

Another interpretive approach seeks to find solutions in modern history. This is the least likely option because it would have been unintelligible to the original hearers and has led to proposals that are quickly disproved. For example, as soon as the European Union had more than ten members, earlier claims that the EU represented the ten horns had to be abandoned.

We know that the vision is heavily symbolic based on the mere facts that the beast both "is" and "is not" at the same time and the entirety of the beast can simply be interpreted as one of the heads. The details are slipperier in this section of Revelation than anywhere else. On the one hand, I am happy to admit that I don't know the best way to interpret these verses, and I would advise you to be suspicious of someone who claims to have it all figured out. On the other hand, there are some clues. The number seven in Revelation consistently points toward wholeness and completion. The number ten has a similar signification. Numbers in Revelation are almost never literal, and even when they are (as in seven churches) there is an additional symbolic meaning. It is possible to see the numbers as simply signifying the fullness or wholeness of oppressive power throughout history. This is suggested by the parallel battle scenes of 16:13–14 and 19:19, where these ten kings are described as the kings of the whole earth; they are not just ten in number. Daniel's four beasts had a cumulative number of seven heads (Dan 7:1–8) and represented four nations that spanned hundreds of years.

The idea that the seven, even eight, heads represent oppressive rulers throughout history is strengthened by recognizing a Hebrew poetic device that has been labeled "graded numerical sayings."[1] Proverbs 6:16 provides a classic example: "There are six things that the Lord hates, seven that are an abomination to him." Ecclesiastes 11:2 says, "Give a portion to seven, or even to

---

1. On this see Richard Bauckham, *The Climax of Prophecy: Studies in the Book of Revelation* (Edinburgh: Clark, 1993), 405.

eight, for you know not what disaster may happen on earth." Micah 5:5 states, "We will raise against him seven shepherds and eight princes of men." These examples are close parallels to the addition of an eighth king to the seven even though it does not naturally arise from the original symbol of a beast with seven heads. The point is not the literal number eight but that seven, even eight, brings a sense of fullness, completion, and finality to the symbol.

The description of the beast as "was, and is not, and is about to rise from the bottomless pit and go to destruction" (Rev 17:8) seems to be an intentional parody of the description of God throughout Revelation as the one "who is and who was and who is to come" (1:4). While God comes to establish his eternal kingdom, the beast comes only to go to destruction. This description of the beast functions to mock or taunt it by reminding it of its final end. Even though it has authority, for a time, over the nations of the world and the physical power to persecute and harm God's people, it will not last forever.

The first readers would have easily understood both the beast and the prostitute as different expressions of Roman power and oppression in the first century, but such an interpretation does not exhaust the symbols. The Lamb is ruling in heaven, and his bride is active on earth, during the entire period between the first and second comings, and this suggests the same for the beast and prostitute, the satanically empowered counterparts and opponents to the Lamb and bride.

John proceeds to briefly describe the final battle, which was already narrated in the sixth and seventh bowl judgments. The ten kings (horns of the beast) join with the beast and make war on the Lamb, but "the Lamb will conquer them, for he is Lord of lords and King of kings, and those with him are called and chosen and faithful" (Rev 17:14). If you remember the discussion of the beast in Revelation 13, you will recall that the "whole earth marveled as they followed the beast ... and they worshiped the beast, saying, 'Who is like the beast, and who can fight against it?'" (vv. 3-4). We finally get to hear a direct answer to that question. The Lamb is greater than the beast and is more than capable of waging war against it.

THE DESTRUCTION OF BABYLON

John briefly moves us back in time, to before the Lamb conquers the beast at the second coming, to describe how evil turns on itself and self-destructs. We are told that God put it into the hearts of the ten kings and the beast to turn on the prostitute, the great city ruling the kings of the earth, and destroy it (Rev 17:16–17). Despite all the wrath and power of the spiritual and physical forces opposing God and his people, they are ultimately powerless to oppose his purposes. The Roman Empire came close to self-destructing in the famous year of four emperors (AD 69). There was near constant civil war, and the future of the empire was at stake. The first readers likely would have looked back at those events as a model for understanding how God's adversaries would in the future destroy themselves from within.

The imagery used to describe the destruction of Babylon the Great is graphic and severe, but it is important to remember that she is not a real person but a symbolic representative of a cultural, religious, and economic system opposed to God and his people. The vision does not promote hatred or abuse of women.

THE DESTRUCTION OF BABYLON (AGAIN)

Revelation 18 is unlike any other chapter in Revelation. John hears various voices celebrating or commenting on the destruction of Babylon and sees those who were seduced by the prostitute mourning her destruction. These include the kings of the earth, the merchants of the earth, and the shipmasters and sailors. Many of the laments John hears are drawn from Old Testament descriptions of the destruction of other powerful cities throughout history, such as Sodom, Gomorrah, Babylon, Tyre, Nineveh, Edom, and even Jerusalem. Babylon the Great symbolizes the seductive, oppressive, and exploitative power of the great cities throughout history.

Revelation 18 does not move the narrative forward but reflects on the destruction of Babylon the Great, which has just been described in chapter 17. Even though it is primarily repetitive, as usual in Revelation, there are unique perspectives and details provided by the parallel visions.

First, the vision confronts us with principle 1 (focus on the original intent of the visions). John hears a voice from heaven directly address God's people: "Come out of her, my people, lest you take part in her sins, lest you share in her plagues; for her sins are heaped high as heaven, and God has remembered her iniquities" (Rev 18:4–5). We are never left for long in Revelation without being directly challenged to respond to the visions. The visions are not intended to simply give us information about the future, but they call on us to act in the present time in light of what we learn about the future. There is a very real danger for God's people to be seduced by Babylon, to pursue luxury and prosperity at the cost of faithfulness. God calls his people to leave Babylon. We cannot, of course, physically leave the world, so we should understand this call as a warning to avoid compromise with the ruling economic, cultural, and religious systems.

Second, her crimes are described in various ways throughout the chapter. In particular, John exposes and critiques Babylon's oppression of people through slavery. John ends a long list of cargo sold to the city by noting "slaves [bodies], that is, human souls" (v. 13). The earliest Christians had no political power to change the laws governing slavery, but they knew that every human being was made in God's image. Human beings were not animals to be bought and sold like cattle, sheep, and horses; they possessed souls. Revelation 18 ends by highlighting the fact that "all nations were deceived by your sorcery. And in her was found the blood of prophets and of saints, and of all who have been slain on earth" (vv. 23–24). She is guilty not only of the persecution of Christians but also of the blood of everyone who has been unjustly slain throughout the world. This alerts us to the fact that Babylon, as a symbol, includes and goes beyond any particular historical city. Babylon is responsible for global deception, oppression, exploitation, and murder.

Third, the judgment of Babylon is presented as God's answer to the prayers of his people for justice in the fifth seal (6:9–11). God's people are called to "Rejoice over her, O heaven, and you saints and apostles and prophets, for God has given judgment for you against her!" (18:20). More explicitly, Revelation 19:2 uses the same language of the prayer from the fifth seal when it states, "For he has judged the great prostitute who corrupted the earth with her immorality, and has *avenged* on her the blood of his servants." This is the judicial vengeance for which God's people have prayed and longed for centuries. How long until God acts to end oppression, murder, exploitation, and evil in his creation? John's vision of Babylon's destruction promises that God will indeed act once and for all to set things right. As we wait for that day, we need the message woven throughout the book of Revelation: It will not be easy, and there will be temptation and opposition along the way, but we must overcome through repentance, faithful endurance, witness, worship, and obedience until the end!

CONCLUSION

Even though some of the details in the vision of the beast in Revelation 17 are hard to pin down, the main points of chapters 17–18 are clear. Babylon the Great helps the dragon and the beasts in their war against God's people throughout history. She represents religious, economic, and cultural seduction and corresponds to the rival Christian leaders (such as Jezebel) who tried to get Christians to compromise in order to avoid persecution. This was the main danger confronting the churches in the seven proclamations (Rev 2–3), and now we are able to identify the demonic power behind this false teaching. Against pressure to compromise with society in order to fit in, avoid persecution and ridicule, and get ahead financially, John's visions seek to motivate us to faithfulness no matter the cost.

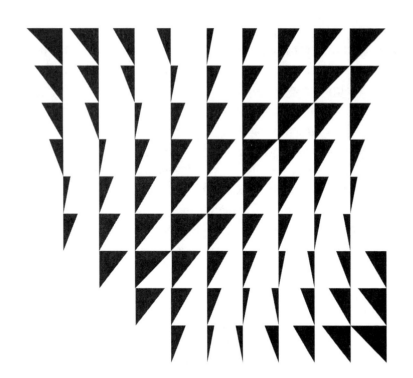

CHAPTER 14

The Second Coming, Millennium,
and Final Judgment

REVELATION 19—20

The long wait is almost over. As early as Revelation 6, we had a vision of the end, the great and final day of the Lord. But the visions kept coming. Every time we thought we reached the end, more visions followed. Visions of evil, oppression, and suffering contrasted with visions of God's judgments and his people in victory. We are now drawing near to the end for the last time. The dragon who has been active behind the scenes the whole time is about to be dealt with forever.

REJOICING IN HEAVEN

Like a bad penny that keeps turning up, we are not yet finished with Babylon the Great. Revelation 18 provided laments from the perspective of those who compromised with Babylon the Great. Their prosperity, hope, and security were tied to her, and without her, they have nothing left. Revelation 19 shows the response of God's people, and the contrast is not subtle. Mourning is replaced with celebration and praise!

The hymns of praise in 19:1–10 are punctuated with cries of "Hallelujah." This is based on a Hebrew imperative that means "Praise Yah[weh]." The expression calls on God's people to join in joyful praise to God. The hymns celebrate God's justice in bringing salvation through judgment: "Salvation and glory and power belong to our God, for his judgments are true and just" (vv. 1–2). He is just because "he has judged the great prostitute who corrupted the earth with her immorality" (v. 2). Babylon the Great not only persecuted God's people but actively corrupted the entire earth, all of humanity, with immorality. Based on the earlier descriptions of Babylon the Great, this immorality includes sexual immorality, religious corruption, and economic exploitation.

Seeing the Big Picture

- Revelation 19 concludes the judgment of Babylon the Great by showing the response of God's people: celebration and praise. It also provides the most explicit description of Jesus's second coming in Revelation.

- Revelation 20 describes the millennium, the final defeat of Satan, and the final judgment. Although these events have been described at various points earlier in Revelation, these are the final and fullest visions of God's people in victory and rest, the final battle, and the final judgment.

The celebration continues as the great prostitute is contrasted with the pure bride. God's people have resisted the seduction of the prostitute, and the Lamb's bride is clothed with the righteous deeds of the saints (vv. 7–8). This signifies that the bride is a corporate way to describe God's united people. This also matches how Paul describes the church as the bride (Eph 5:22–32). The grammar of Revelation 19:8 highlights both God's grace and human choices. They merge together seamlessly and are not in conflict with each other. The bride's clothing is the righteous deeds of the saints, so their choices and decisions matter. Our actions are not unimportant. This does not lead to a works-based salvation, however, because "it was granted her to clothe herself" (v. 8). God enables what he requires, and our ability to overcome is the result not of unaided grit and determination but of God's gracious gift.

With Babylon removed from the earth, it is time for the "marriage of the Lamb" (v. 7). The bride is ready, people have been invited, and all that is needed is the coming of the Lamb. Before describing the Lamb's coming, John records a somewhat embarrassing personal account. He attempts to worship his angelic guide but is quickly rebuked: "You must not do that! ... Worship God" (v. 10). This highlights the fact that none of us is immune to the danger of misplaced worship. Only God and the Lamb are worthy of our worship and allegiance.

THE SECOND COMING

John next sees heaven opened and Jesus on a white horse (19:11). Jesus is described as "Faithful and True," "the Word of God," and "King of kings and Lord of lords" (vv. 11, 13, 16). He will judge and make war in righteousness, rule the nations, and "tread the winepress of the fury of the wrath of God the Almighty" (vv. 11, 15). The allusion to Psalm 2:7–9 ("he will rule them with a rod of iron") identifies him as the Messiah and the child of the woman from Revelation 12:5. There, Jesus is enthroned in heaven, while here, he is fulfilling his destiny to physically and concretely rule the nations of the earth.

It is hard to know the significance of his robe dipped in blood. Is it his own blood (signifying his sacrificial death) or the blood of his enemies? The blood of the Lamb is connected to his sacrificial death in many places in Revelation and is the main key to his and our victory (1:5; 5:9; 7:14; 12:11). The vision of the grape harvest and the treading of the winepress of God's wrath also features more blood than ever seen in any Hollywood horror movie (14:20; 19:15). It is probably significant that the robe is dipped in blood before the battle starts; this links his victory to his own sacrificial death. Jesus absorbed the violence of evil directed against himself before bringing violence in justice against evil.

This second coming must be seen in parallel to earlier descriptions of the final battle.

Rev 16:13-14	Rev 17:14	Rev 19:19-20
And I saw, coming out of the mouth of the dragon and out of the mouth of the beast and out of the mouth of the false prophet, three unclean spirits like frogs. For they are demonic spirits, performing signs, who go abroad to the kings of the whole world, *to assemble them for battle* on the great day of God the Almighty.	They [the beast and the ten kings] will *make war* on the Lamb, and the Lamb will conquer them, for he is Lord of lords and King of kings, and those with him are called and chosen and faithful.	And I saw the beast and the kings of the earth with their armies *gathered to make war* against him who was sitting on the horse and against his army. And the beast was captured, and with it the false prophet ... These two were thrown alive into the lake of fire that burns with sulfur.

The battle in each vision involves the beasts with the kings of the earth in opposition to God and the Lamb. As usual in Revelation, even though the visions describe the same events, they each provide unique details and perspectives; they are not boring and predictable reduplications. Revelation 16 does not narrate the conclusion of the battle or mention the Lamb; instead, it skips to the final judgment in the seventh bowl judgment. Chapters 17 and 19 both focus on the fact that this final conflict involves the second coming of Jesus to personally defeat the beast. Other smaller differences are present, but the parallels indisputably point to the same event. Jesus does not return three times for three final battles. He returns once at the end of history to finally and permanently remove evil from his creation.

The descriptions of the battle in Revelation 17 and 19 show that Jesus will be accompanied by his called, chosen, and faithful people (17:14; 19:14). Despite the fact that they join the Lamb for the conflict, they do not do any fighting. The enemies are defeated by Jesus's spoken word, which is symbolized by a sword coming out of his mouth. This describes not a literal battle at a specific place with physical weapons but rather the final attempt of God's adversaries to wipe his people off the face of the earth through intense global persecution and temptation. God's people are presented as an army engaged in holy war, but the battle is fought through faithfulness, witness, and worship. God's people are never depicted in Revelation as engaged in violent fighting for their faith. They are a pacifist army that gains its victory through bearing witness to the truth to the point of death.

Rev 19:17-18, 21	Ezek 39:4, 17-20
Then I saw an angel standing in the sun, and with a loud voice he called to all the birds that fly directly overhead, "Come, gather for the great supper of God, to eat the flesh of kings, the flesh of captains, the flesh of mighty men, the flesh of horses and their riders, and the flesh of all men, both free and slave, both small and great." ... And the rest were slain by the sword that came from the mouth of him who was sitting on the horse, and all the birds were gorged with their flesh.	You shall fall on the mountains of Israel, you and all your hordes and the peoples who are with you. I will give you to birds of prey of every sort and to the beasts of the field to be devoured. ... As for you, son of man, thus says the Lord God: Speak to the birds of every sort and to all beasts of the field: "Assemble and come, gather from all around to the sacrificial feast that I am preparing for you, a great sacrificial feast on the mountains of Israel, and you shall eat flesh and drink blood. You shall eat the flesh of the mighty, and drink the blood of the princes of the earth—of rams, of lambs, and of he-goats, of bulls, all of them fat beasts of Bashan. And you shall eat fat till you are filled, and drink blood till you are drunk, at the sacrificial feast that I am preparing for you. And you shall be filled at my table with horses and char- ioteers, with mighty men and all kinds of warriors," declares the Lord God.

The main Old Testament prophecy John uses to describe this final battle is the prophecy about Gog and Magog in Ezekiel 38–39. There are several parallels, but the most obvious one focuses on the supper.

The next time you read Ezekiel 38–39, you no longer need to wonder what it is describing. John's visions in Revelation show us that at least some of the first Christians understood Ezekiel 38–39 to refer to the second coming.

Finally, notice that there are two suppers recorded in Revelation 19. This is not accidental: the marriage supper of the Lamb is contrasted with the great supper of God's judgment. Those invited to the marriage supper of the Lamb will celebrate and be at peace, while those who attend the other supper will find themselves to be the main course for vultures. The main point is clear: make sure to be at the right supper! Don't ally with the beast through compromise and misplaced worship. The beast and false prophet (second beast) are "thrown alive into the lake of fire that burns with sulfur" (v. 20).

THE MILLENNIUM

John then sees a vision of Satan being bound and imprisoned in the abyss for a thousand years, while those who had been killed for their witness come to life and reign on earth for a thousand years. This millennial vision has been the most debated in the entire book of Revelation. The position known as premillennialism holds that Jesus comes back before a literal millennium takes place, while amillennial interpretations hold that the millennium does not literally take place after Jesus returns but describes some aspect of spiritual reality throughout history (either the spiritual resurrection that takes place when people become Christians or the intermediate state of deceased believers between death and resurrection life in God's new creation). As far back as we can tell in church history, Christians were debating whether this was a literal thousand-year reign on earth. Good and faithful Christians have been on both sides of this debate from at least the early second century until today. This reality should give us some interpretive humility, and one's view of the millennium should not be used to exclude people from Christian ministry or fellowship. No significant point of Christian teaching depends on the millennium, and we should graciously live in unity with Christians who have different perspectives on this.

My own views have shifted over time, and the more I study Revelation, the more convinced I am that the vision of the millennium describes the intermediate state of believers at rest between Jesus's first and second comings. The visions throughout Revelation have alternated back and forth between scenes of conflict and judgment and scenes of God's people in victory and at rest in the intermediate state. Visions of God's people in victory and at rest can be found in 6:9-11; 7:9-17; 11:15-18; 14:1-5, 13; 15:2-4; 19:1-9; and 20:4-6. None of the scenes are exact copies or replicas, but they all point to the same reality. The visions in Revelation 21-22 focus exclusively on resurrection life in God's new creation, but the rest of the visions primarily focus on the intermediate state of believers between their death and future resurrection. These visions of the intermediate state in Revelation often contain details related to both the intermediate state of believers in heaven with God and their eternal rule on earth following resurrection and the final judgment; the line between them is often fuzzy.

The transition between Revelation 19 and 20 ("Then I saw") does not require a chronological relationship. John sees and puts his visions in a particular order, but it is rarely chronological, and later visions often repeat earlier ones. The specific number, one thousand, also does not require a literal interpretation because numbers are almost always symbolic in apocalyptic literature. Some people argue that a literal millennium is necessary for God to fulfill his promises to ethnic Israel about their restoration to the land of Israel, but this explanation is highly unlikely for at least three reasons. First, there is nothing in the millennium vision itself to suggest that it is focused on ethnic Jews as opposed to all of God's people who have been killed for their witness. Second, John applies Old Testament passages about the restoration of Israel either to God's people in the present time (comprised of Jews and gentiles) or, in 21–22, to resurrection life in God's new creation. Third, John does not use the millennial vision to illustrate the fulfillment of Old Testament promises about ethnic Israel. He instead uses it to highlight the great reversal that takes place when God's people are killed for their faith. They are put to death in shame and derision, but their faithful death results in victory and life. This is the point of all of the visions of victory and rest throughout Revelation. God's people are vindicated: they have been oppressed, persecuted, and killed throughout history but have faithfully persevered and are rewarded. Several passages in Revelation anticipate that God's people will reign on the earth in the future (2:26–27; 3:21; 5:10; 20:6), but these references are fulfilled through resurrection life in God's new creation (22:5).

The binding of Satan refers to the effects of Jesus's first coming: his ministry, death, resurrection, and enthronement. Satan is bound and limited until the very end, but he is not completely inactive. This binding corresponds to how he was defeated in heaven and cast down to earth in Revelation 12:7–12; note how he is described as the dragon, the ancient serpent, the devil, and Satan only in 12:9 and 20:2. John wants us to read these events together. Satan lost significant authority and power when he was forcibly thrown from heaven to earth because of Jesus's first coming, but he is still able to empower beasts to afflict Christians. The idea that Satan has been bound because of Jesus's first coming is common throughout the New Testament. Jesus taught that he had bound the strong man (Satan) and was plundering his house (Matt 12:28–29; Mark 3:26–27; Luke 11:20–22). Jesus elsewhere attributes his followers' power to cast out demonic beings to the fact that Satan fell from heaven (Luke 10:17–19). In John's Gospel, Jesus proclaims, "Now is the judgment of this world; now will the ruler of this world be cast out" (John 12:31). Jesus connects both the binding of Satan and his fall from heaven to his own earthly ministry.

Paul likewise was convinced that Jesus's first coming "disarmed the rulers and authorities and put them to open shame" (Col 2:15) and that the "man of lawlessness" was currently being restrained (2 Thess 2:1–12). Satan's fall and binding do not mean that he is completely inactive because demons were and are active in the world; it simply means that Jesus and his followers have power over demonic spiritual beings. The binding or falling represents the decisive breaking of Satan's power, even though he can still cause a lot of mischief. His remaining power is not sufficient to accuse God's people or destroy the woman in Revelation 12, but he does empower the beasts to persecute and kill God's people on earth in chapter 13, and right before the end, he will be enabled to deceive the whole world in preparation for the final battle, the final global attempt to destroy God's people.

One's interpretation of the millennium will also depend on how one interprets the last battle of Revelation 20:7–10.

THE LAST LAST BATTLE

John's next vision describes what happens when Satan is released and allowed to deceive the nations. He gathers Gog and Magog, an uncountable multitude, to surround God's people and the beloved city. The battle seems to end before it even begins, and fire falls from heaven to consume them. The devil is then thrown into the lake of fire with the beast and false prophet to be tormented forever. Satan is not the ruler or king of Hell; he is its prisoner.

The key question should be evident: is this a second last battle, or is it another description of the last battle that has already been narrated in the sixth bowl judgment (16:12–16), in 17:13–14, and in 19:11–21? There are several indications that this is directly parallel to the other descriptions of the last battle and should not be seen as a separate event or a second last battle. The different accounts are not direct copycats, and each one provides unique details and perspectives. The battles in Revelation 17 and 19 focus on the conflict between the beast and the Lamb. The battle in Revelation 20 focuses on the battle between the dragon and God (Jesus is not mentioned). Importantly, the sixth bowl judgment indicates that both the dragon and the beast were together when they deceived the nations to come to the war (16:13). The last battle of the sixth bowl judgment is thus further described in chapters 17 and 19 as a battle between the beast and the Lamb and in chapter 20 as a battle between the dragon and God. They are not separate battles but different perspectives on the same battle.

Other parallels cannot be overlooked. When discussing the battle in Revelation 16 and 19 above, we noted that the visions of Gog and Magog in Ezekiel 38-39 were significant Old Testament precedents. The battle in Revelation 20 makes this connection explicit by actually mentioning Gog and Magog. The battles of Revelation 16, 19, and 20 are all visionary interpretations and applications of the battle in Ezekiel 38-39.

Those who do not find these observations convincing have many additional theological questions to answer. Why is Satan bound only to be released again? Why are the nations protected from Satan's deception at the beginning of Revelation 20, right after they had all been destroyed and eaten by birds at the end of Revelation 19? Who are the deceived nations at the end of the millennium? Over whom do the saints rule during the millennium? How will it work out for resurrected people to live alongside non-resurrected people in the old, untransformed world for a thoussnd years? Why does the Bible nowhere else speak of two separate physical resurrections for God's people? These questions are not insurmountable, and hypothetical answers could be given. If there were not a better alternative, Bible-believing Christians should hold to a literal millennium, no matter how many strange questions it raised. The problem is that there is a better interpretive option that makes good sense of the vision within the book of Revelation as a whole. Remember principle 3: recognize repetition.

There is much more that can be said on the millennial debate, and whole books have been written just on the millennial vision, but this is not the place for that kind of discussion. I am convinced that a careful reading of Revelation leads to an amillennial position, but I also greatly appreciate and value those who disagree. The good news is that principle 1 (focus on the original purpose of the visions) is not affected by the debate, and Christians with both views can encourage each other to overcome through repentance, worship, witness, faithfulness, and obedience until Jesus returns.

THE FINAL JUDGMENT

After Satan is thrown into the lake of fire, John sees his last vision of the final judgment. He sees God's throne, before which earth and sky flee away. This cosmic upheaval alerts us to the connection of the final judgment to the sixth seal (6:14) and seventh bowl judgment (16:20). The seventh trumpet also describes the judgment of the dead (11:18). This last vision of the final judgment, however, is much more detailed and explicit. John sees the dead, great and small, standing before the throne. The dead are judged by what is written in the books based on what they had done in life. If anyone's name is not found written in the book of life, they are cast into the lake of fire. The plural books and the singular book of life symbolize God's knowledge and his verdict. Some interpreters draw a distinction between this judgment and a separate judgment for Christians, but all the different biblical texts simply look forward to a single final judgment; no single passage in the New Testament describes two judgments. Each individual human being will stand before God, and their fate will be determined by what they did and whether their name is in the book of life. Between the two, the book of life is determinative.

Someone may be a generally pleasant and good person (at least compared with most other people), but that will not be sufficient in the final judgment if their name is not written in the book of life. In the vision, the book of life trumps the books of works, but the books are not pitted against each other in that way. Both verdicts converge on each person. Jesus makes it clear that he will judge his people based on their works: "And all the churches will know that I am he who searches mind and heart, and I will give to each of you according to your works" (Rev 2:23). John is not presenting a works-based salvation because it is only the Lamb's blood that frees us from our sins (1:5), purifies us (7:14), and enables us to overcome (12:11). This does not give us freedom to sin, however, because Jesus also warns that those who do not overcome risk having their names blotted from the book of life (3:5). In theological terms, John does not pit justification and sanctification against each other as if they were in conflict; both are involved in overcoming, both are God's gracious gift, and both are necessary for final salvation. The fact that the verdicts from the books of works and the book of life are not at odds with each other does not require a standard of perfection—the first step to overcoming is repentance, and God's people are called to repentance whenever they recognize that they have fallen short along the way. The goal is not perfection but repentance, and in Revelation, genuine repentance is linked to transformation. God's overcoming people live differently from the world around them in the visions of Revelation; this is nonnegotiable.

CONCLUSION

With Revelation 19-20, we come to the end for the last time. Jesus returns to defeat the beasts and the dragon forever. God himself presides over the final judgment, and his knowledge and assessment of each person determines their fate. The names of those who overcome will be found in the Lamb's book of life. Their names were written in the book before the foundation of the world (Rev 13:8; 17:8) and were not blotted out of it (3:5).

These final visions of judgment are likely meant to elicit certain emotions. The hymns of Revelation 19 lead us into celebration, praise, and thanksgiving as we recognize that God has acted at last to rescue his people from suffering and oppression and to judge and remove evil from his creation. The visions should also instill in us a healthy fear. We will stand before God one day and give an account for our lives. We do not live in terror of that day because of our allegiance to the Lamb, but our healthy fear should motivate us to avoid sin, compromise, and idolatry the way we would avoid drinking poison, playing with a venomous snake, or dancing on the edge of a cliff.

The visions also produce confidence in us regarding the future. We do not know what might happen in our personal lives or families. Will we be subject to persecution or ridicule? Will we experience debilitating sickness or extreme poverty? Will a loved one die suddenly in an accident? We do not know the future, and we are not promised safety in this life. We have confidence, however, that no matter what happens to us, we will share in Jesus's victory over both the first, physical death and the second, spiritual death. We may not be safe, but we are secure.

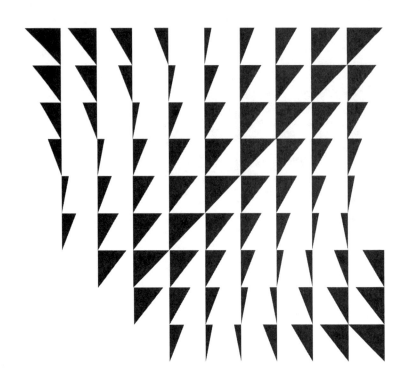

CHAPTER 15

New Heavens and New Earth

We have come to the end at last. Our journey through the visions of Revelation may have occasionally felt troubling and difficult. The visions are not comfortable, and they were not meant to be. They were meant to challenge us, shake us awake, and motivate us to costly and sacrificial action. The visions contain repeated images of judgment, suffering, and persecution. You may have experienced reader's whiplash as you were thrown from visions of victory to judgment to persecution and then back again. You likely experienced at least some déjà vu as each successive vision provided new perspectives and details regarding the basic storyline.

Many readers find these final two chapters to be their favorite. The closing chapters are joyful and comforting. They provide an inspiring picture of God's new creation that fills us with longing and desire. We want to be there. We want to experience that life now. We want all the sorrow and suffering of this life to be washed away. As we put the Bible down, however, we are quickly confronted with the reality that we are not there yet. We are in the

179

three-and-a-half-years during which the beast has authority to deceive the world and persecute Christians and when Babylon the Great is getting drunk on the blood of those who dwell on the earth.

God provides these visions of the end in Revelation 21–22 to inspire us and give us the confidence that it will be worth it in the end if we do not give up. Evil and chaos will not have the final word.

Seeing the Big Picture

- Revelation 21–22 provides two separate visions of resurrection life in God's new creation. These visions conclude Revelation and function as the ending of the entire Christian Bible.

- The concluding visions fill us with hope and confidence about the future and motivate us to faithfully overcome no matter the cost.

NEW CREATION (REVELATION 21:1—8)

John's first words set the stage for the vision as whole: he sees a new heaven and a new earth. Interpreters debate whether this is an entirely new earth. The Bible as a whole leads us to expect this new earth to be a renewed and restored version of the current world. Our future existence will not be as disembodied spirits floating around in space; it is much more concrete and physical than that. We will have resurrected physical bodies to live in a physical world. The fact that John does not see a sea in this new earth should not lead us to think that God's new creation will not have large bodies of water similar to today's oceans and seas. The sea was widely seen in antiquity as a symbol and the source of evil, chaos, danger, and disorder. This is suggested by the fact that the sea is the source of the beast in Revelation 13:1. God does not hate large bodies of water; the lack of the sea rather suggests the removal of evil, suffering, chaos, danger, and disorder.

John next sees the new Jerusalem coming down from heaven. The symbol of the new Jerusalem is multifaceted. It is identified as the wife, the bride of the Lamb (21:9); this closely connects it with God's people and suggests that it represents people and not physical space. As the vision progresses, however, many details indicate that it is a physical place. Its dimensions (12,000 stadia or

1,380 miles in each direction) are such that it would cover more or
less the entire known world of the time. The dimensions are not
literal, however, because its height would be far too great. There
is no fixed line between earth and space, but it is widely accepted
that space begins at roughly 62 miles above sea level, and this city
would extend upward for 1,380 miles! The metaphorical dimensions suggest that it would encompass the entire earth. Its cubic
shape further indicates that it is the holy of holies (21:16). With
the descent of the new Jerusalem, God's heavenly throne room has
come down to earth, and there is a perfect blending of the physical
and spiritual worlds. There is currently a separation between the
two, but in God's new creation, the spiritual and physical worlds
will be united. The symbol of the New Jerusalem thus suggests
a blending of God's realm and our realm in such a way that he
directly dwells among his people; this dwelling among us encom-
passes the entire world.

John makes this interpretation explicit when he notes, "Behold,
the dwelling place of God is with man. He will dwell with them,
and they will be his people, and God himself will be with them as
their God" (21:3). The promise that God will dwell with his people
draws from Old Testament covenantal promises God made to his
people; John sees those promises as reaching final and complete
fulfillment in the future. Certainly, we have access to God through
Jesus in prayer and worship right now in the present age, but there
is still a physical distance. This distance will someday be removed.

Revelation 21:4 presents what is perhaps the most intimate
picture of God in the entire Bible. God "will wipe away every tear
from their eyes." God will not be distant or frightening. He will
be close enough to touch each person. When he touches them, he
will not destroy them; he will, rather, personally and individually
wipe the tears from their eyes. John further explains: "Death shall
be no more, neither shall there be mourning, nor crying, nor pain
anymore, for the former things have passed away" (21:4). Sin and
death are regularly presented throughout the New Testament as

the greatest enemies of mankind. In John's visions, sin has been decisively dealt with by the Lamb's blood (1:5), and death will not be allowed into God's new creation. The language is similar to the way the sea was described a few verses earlier: nothing that disrupts human flourishing and joy will exist anymore! God's personal presence and care is the guarantee.

The last verses of the first vision of new creation stress principle 1 (focus on the original purpose). God speaks to his people in the first person and assures them that the one who conquers or overcomes will inherit everything that has just been described (21:7). The whole book is designed to motivate us to overcome in life no matter the cost, and these final visions continue that focus. The next verse makes it clear, however, that not everyone will overcome or take part in the fulfillment of humanity's purpose and goal. Some will be excluded: "But as for the cowardly, the faithless, the detestable, as for murderers, the sexually immoral, sorcerers, idolaters, and all liars, their portion will be in the lake that burns with fire and sulfur, which is the second death" (21:8). The lake of fire is the location of the beasts (19:20), the dragon (20:10), Death and Hades (20:14), and those whose names are not in the Lamb's book of life (20:15). It is possible that the lake of fire is a literal place, but it is also possibly a symbolic description of exclusion from God and from God's new creation. This does not make it less frightening since symbols still point to very real realities. Not everyone will experience resurrection life in God's new creation; some will instead suffer God's punishment.

THE NEW JERUSALEM (REVELATION 21:9—22:5)

The second vision of the new Jerusalem parallels the first vision but gives additional details and perspectives. This follows John's normal pattern of using multiple visions to describe the same reality and time period—in this case, resurrection life in God's new creation. The additional details stress safety and protection. The city has huge walls, but the gates are never shut (21:25). They are never shut because there is no night or danger (21:25). Life is characterized by abundance and prosperity; the city is described with images of unparalleled wealth. The names on the gates and foundations stress the unity of God's people in the Old and New Testaments (21:12-14); there is a shared destination for all of God's true people throughout history. The dimensions are all related to twelve or multiples of twelve. There are twelve gates and twelve foundations, the walls are 144 cubits high, and the city is a cube of 12,000 stadia. The multiples of twelve remind us of how God's people are described as 144,000 in 7:4 and 14:1. The number twelve comes from the twelve tribes of Israel, and twelve times twelve stresses the unity of God's people in the Old and New Testaments.

It is a multiethnic city where God's people from every nation have a home (21:24-26). This incredibly joyous and celebratory vision is interrupted by a reminder of those who are excluded: "But nothing unclean will ever enter it, nor anyone who does what is detestable or false, but only those who are written in the Lamb's book of life" (21:27). This reminder further motivates us as God's people to overcome through repentance, worship, witness, obedience, and perseverance.

John's vision of new creation, the new heavens and earth, in 21:9–22:5, seems to be in large part an interpretation and application of Ezekiel's visions of restoration (Ezek 40-48). Many parallels support this connection (see, in particular, Ezek 40:2, 3, 5-6; 41:4, 5; 42:15-20; 43:2-5; 45:2; 47:1, 9, 12; 48:8-13, 16-17, 30-34 with Rev 21:10–22:2). The main differences between the two visionary accounts result from the lack of a temple in John's vision (21:22). The temple in Ezekiel is replaced by the entire new Jerusalem, which represents the Holy of Holies encompassing the entire known world. John's vision of the city takes up details from both the temple and city in Ezekiel's visions. If you read Ezekiel 40-48 without the insight of John's vision, you will end up with many interpretive questions: will Ezekiel's visions be fulfilled in a literal and physical way in history or at the end of history? John helps us out tremendously, showing us that the visions in Ezekiel 40–48 will be fulfilled in God's eternal new creation. John does *not* apply Ezekiel's visions to the millennium or to a rebuilt physical temple in history.

Finally, God's new creation is pictured as a reversal of the fall and the curses of Genesis 3. It will be a restoration of all that was lost when humanity originally rebelled against God. In Genesis 3:22–24, humanity is barred from access to the tree of life, but in God's new creation, our access to it will be restored, and the leaves of the tree will bring healing to humanity (Rev 22:2). Genesis 3 records that humanity's rejection of God's rule in the garden brought curses on human beings and creation. The world became a broken place filled with broken people. John's final vision shows the restoration of God's creation and of humanity. In God's new creation, there will be no more curse (22:3).

Just as the first humans walked with God in a creation that was undamaged by rebellion and sin, John notes that God's people will "see his face" (22:4). We know that in the present time, no one can see God's face and live, but in God's new creation, we will see him and live. Unlike some depictions of heaven as a boring place where people sit on clouds and strum on harps for all eternity, Revelation presents a much more dynamic picture: God's people "will reign forever and ever" (22:5). God originally created us as his image bearers to represent him and extend his rule and reign throughout his creation (Gen 1:26–28). Because of sin and death, we are unable to fulfill that purpose; we are incapable of accomplishing the purpose for which we were created. In God's future new creation, however, we will finally be able to fulfill that purpose. John doesn't give us details, but it is a big universe, and we certainly will not be bored.

THE EPILOGUE (REVELATION 22:6—21)

Several themes come together in Revelation's conclusion. A blessing is pronounced on "the one who keeps the words of the prophecy of this book" (22:7). This blessing matches the similar blessing at the start of the book (1:3) and functions to remind us of the main point: keep the words of the book! The visions of Revelation function as a call to action.

The accompanying angel instructs John not to seal up the words of the prophecy of the book because the time was near (22:10). This contrasts with the explanation given to Daniel that "the words are shut up and sealed until the time of the end" (Dan 12:9). For John, the end had begun with the enthronement of Jesus at God's right hand, and God's final judgments were beginning to be poured out on the earth.

The final blessing of the book is paired with a reminder that some would remain excluded. The lake of fire imagery is dropped here in favor of an image of exclusion. They are kept outside the city: "Blessed are those who wash their robes, so that they may have the right to the tree of life and that they may enter the city by the gates. Outside are the dogs and sorcerers and the sexually immoral and murderers and idolaters, and everyone who loves and practices falsehood" (22:14-15).

The final warning in Revelation focuses on those who might add to or subtract from John's visions (22:18-19). This warning technically applies only to the book of Revelation, but once Revelation was included as the final book in the Christian Bible, it is regularly understood as applying to the entire Bible.

This final section of Revelation stresses the source of John's message: he is communicating Jesus's message to his people (22:12, 16). Jesus is coming soon (22:12, 20). Two thousand years and counting may not feel very soon, but 2 Peter 3:8 reminds us of the fact that we do not experience time in the same way that God does, and many of Jesus's parables stress the fact that even if there is a long delay before he returns, we need to remain ready at any moment. The declaration of Jesus's coming soon has rightly led Christians from the first century until today to expect his coming within their generation. It rightly leads to an attitude of constant expectation that motivates us to stay alert, awake, and active.

Revelation ends with a closing prayer. "Come, Lord Jesus! The grace of the Lord Jesus be with all. Amen" (22:20–21). The world is a broken place, and the dragon, the beasts, and Babylon are still actively opposing God and his people. In the midst of this brokenness and conflict, we are called to actively resist until the end of our lives or until Jesus comes. This final prayer expresses a deep Christian longing: "Come, Lord Jesus!"

CONCLUSION

These concluding visions are not included just to give us information about the future; they are intended to affect us in meaningful ways. They provide comfort, motivation, warning, and invitation. They comfort us by reminding us that no matter how hard life gets, the future will be better. The God who does not lie has promised, and we base our lives on his faithfulness. They motivate us by giving us vivid glimpses of our future destiny. They warn us by reminding us that some will be excluded; not everyone will be saved. When we are tempted to compromise with sin, we need to hear these warnings and allow them to motivate us to overcome evil. They also invite us and every human being to come and be a part of God's new creation. God is not trying to keep people out; the invitation is for all who are thirsty. "And let the one who is thirsty come; let the one who desires take the water of life without price" (22:17). Are you thirsty today? Do you recognize your spiritual need? The price has been paid by the Lamb, and God invites you to join him in his plans for the future. The future begins now, and Revelation confronts us with a question of ultimate significance: Will you be an overcomer?

CONCLUSION

Reading Revelation Rightly

We have reached the end of our brief tour of John's visions in Revelation. In Part 1, we considered five foundational interpretive rules for the journey, while in Part 2, we walked through the visions of Revelation from beginning to end. Each chapter sought to illustrate how the five interpretive principles help us understand what Jesus, through John, wanted his people to know and do. In Part 2, it became evident that these principles do not solve all the interpretive difficulties. It also became clear that if you neglect or ignore these principles, you will find yourself lost in a maze of visions with no firm footing and no working compass.

Principle 1 functions as true north; it will guide you properly no matter how disorienting the visions might feel. The book as a whole represents a massive encouragement to overcome, endure, remain faithful, witness, worship, and refuse to compromise. The book motivates this overcoming endurance through visions of the future, God's kingdom, heaven, eternal reward, and the opposite, eternal punishment. God's message to the church comes out loud and clear: You must overcome! Do not grow weary in your obedience and witness! Do not compromise with the sin, lust, and idolatry of your surrounding culture! Overcome!

Principle 2 functions to identify unlikely and implausible interpretations. It is important to begin by seeking to understand how the first hearers would have understood the visions. This will help us determine the originally intended meaning more accurately than if we were to ignore the original historical context and try to interpret the visions solely from our twenty-first-century perspective. Interpretations that try to connect the visions in Revelation to political leaders, geopolitical developments, or technological advancements should be viewed with strong skepticism. The motivational force of the book (principle 1) does not depend on finding correspondences between Revelation and the news of the day.

Principle 3 helps us understand the basic storyline: most of the visions either cover the entire period between Jesus's first and second comings or focus on some aspect of that basic storyline. We join John's first readers within this period of time. It is a time of conflict and temptation, during which the dragon is waging a deadly war against God's people by means of the beasts and Babylon. Christians will suffer for their faith but must overcome through faithful witness and worship.

Principle 4 alerts us to the importance of symbolism in Revelation, but it does not tell us what the symbols mean. The use of images and symbols in the Old Testament, New Testament, and contemporary Jewish literature provides good guidance. Recognizing the symbolic nature of the visions guards us against literalistic interpretations that would have been impossible for John and the first hearers to understand.

Principle 5 draws attention to how Revelation functions as a fitting and beautiful conclusion to the entire biblical narrative. The final visions in Revelation 21–22 show how the problems of sin and death introduced in Genesis 3 are overcome and humanity is finally and fully able to fulfill the purpose for which we were created. This is accomplished through the sacrificial death of the

Lamb, his enthronement at God's right hand, and his victorious
return to fully establish God's rule and reign on earth.

The five principles function together as a pair of interpretive glasses; I hope they have improved your vision. No study of
Revelation can answer every possible question, but this study has
sought to equip you with the tools needed to ask better questions,
seek better answers, and evaluate which proposed interpretations are more or less probable. Moving forward, you can read
the visions with attention to their motivational force, the original
context, the parallels among the visions, the symbolic significance
of imagery, and the broader biblical and theological landscape.

Let me close by suggesting two areas in which Revelation
brings a particularly strong challenge to Christians today. First,
Revelation has a suspicious view of physical wealth. Money, luxury,
and abundance are connected, on the one hand, with injustice
and oppression, and, on the other hand, with complacency and
compromise. John does not explicitly state that Christians cannot
be both wealthy and faithful in this age, but the visions provide
repeated warnings regarding the increased dangers and tempta-
tions of wealth. This is a warning not just to the Western church
but to Christians all over the world who encounter opportunities
to climb the ladder of wealth and prosperity. Poverty is not a virtue,
and wealth can be administered faithfully, but excessive wealth
comes with increased spiritual danger.

Second, Revelation provides a strong critique of human governments and systems of power. In Romans 13, Paul presents a
positive picture of human government and argues that God has
delegated to human rulers the task of carrying out justice in the
world and producing stable societies conducive to human flourishing. Paul, of course, knows that human governments will only ever
do this imperfectly, but it is still the ideal standard against which
governments should be measured. John provides a different perspective and repeatedly links human government with the dragon

and beasts; they are oppressive tools of exploitation, murder, and persecution. Both of these biblical perspectives inform a Christian approach to government and need to be heard. Revelation serves as a warning to Christians against allying too closely with any political party or looking to human political leaders as saviors. Regardless of citizenship or party affiliation, Christians ultimately serve only one king and one kingdom and must constantly resist the temptation to link their allegiance to Christ with their allegiance to human rulers.

These two dangers are not insignificant: "Come out of her, my people, lest you take part in her sins, lest you share in her plagues; for her sins are heaped high as heaven, and God has remembered her iniquities" (Rev 18:4–5). Complicity in oppressive luxury and power is linked with a sharing of punishment. Revelation contains some of the strongest warnings in the Bible. However, these warnings are not the whole picture, and they are balanced with messages of incredible hope, grace, and invitation: "The Spirit and the Bride say, 'Come.' And let the one who hears say, 'Come.' And let the one who is thirsty come; let the one who desires take the water of life without price" (Rev 22:17).

Acknowledgements

I would like to acknowledge and thank all of my students at Tyndale Theological Seminary in Badhoevedorp, the Netherlands between 2013 and 2021. My ideas were shaped over those years of carefully studying the text of Revelation with you in our exegesis classes and morning Greek reading. I will never forget our time spent together in the Greek text; the ideas in this book were presented and discussed many times throughout those years. May God continue to strengthen and guide you through your journey of life and faith. Many thanks are also due to Southeastern Baptist Theological Seminary and their Visiting Scholar Sabbatical Program. The semester I spent with you in the fall of 2018 allowed me the opportunity to put the first five chapters into writing and craft a book proposal. Finally, I would like to thank Derek Brown, my editor at Lexham, who spent meaningful time with me discussing the proposal and providing suggestions for improvement.

For Further Reading

This book has only been able to scratch the surface, and there is much more to learn about the book of Revelation. As evident to those with ears to hear, David A. deSilva, G. K. Beale, and Richard Bauckham have had a significant impact on my interpretation of Revelation, and I would encourage you to start with them. Hopefully, you are ready and eager for the next step. Any of the following books will stimulate and improve your understanding.

Bauckham, Richard. *The Theology of the Book of Revelation.* Cambridge; New York: Cambridge University Press, 1993.

Beale, G.K., with David H. Campbell. *Revelation: A Shorter Commentary.* Grand Rapids: Eerdmans, 2015.

Dalrymple, Rob. *Follow the Lamb: A Guide to Reading, Understanding, and Applying the Book of Revelation.* Bellingham, WA: Lexham, 2019.

deSilva, David A. *Unholy Allegiances: Heeding Revelation's Warning.* Peabody, MA: Hendrickson, 2013.

Duvall, J. Scott. *The Heart of Revelation: Understanding the 10 Essential Themes of the Bible's Final Book.* Nashville: B&H Academic, 2019.

Koester, Craig R. *Revelation and the End of All Things*. Grand Rapids: Eerdmans, 2001.

Kraybill, J. Nelson. *Apocalypse and Allegiance: Worship, Politics, and Devotion in the Book of Revelation*. Grand Rapids: Brazos Press, 2010.

Metzger, Bruce M. *Breaking the Code: Understanding the Book of Revelation*. Nashville; New York: Abingdon, 1993.

Wilson, Mark. *Victory through the Lamb: A Guide to Revelation in Plain Language*. Bellingham, WA: Lexham, 2018.

Wright, N. T. *Revelation for Everyone*. Louisville: Westminster John Knox, 2009.

For those who want to really dive into the details, I recommend the following.

Bauckham, Richard. *The Climax of Prophecy: Studies in the Book of Revelation*. Edinburgh; London; New York: T&T Clark, 1993.

Beale, Gregory K. *The Book of Revelation*. New International Greek Testament Commentary. Grand Rapids: Eerdmans, 1999.

deSilva, David A. *Seeing Things John's Way: The Rhetoric of the Book of Revelation*. Louisville: Westminster John Knox, 2009.

Koester, Craig R. *Revelation: A New Translation with Introduction and Commentary*. New Haven: Yale University Press, 2014.

Subject Index

C

D

H

I

J

R

repentance, 10, 14, 88, 119, 176

repetition, 4, 33-46, 54-55, 190

return, Jesus's. *See* second coming

Revelation (biblical book)

and the Abrahamic promise, 62-66, 111

approaches to interpretation, 1-2

authority, 71-79, 83

biblical context, 55-56, 59-66, 78, 190-91

and chronology, 33-41, 76, 102-3, 110, 122, 129, 148, 155-56, 185

debates about, 9-11

hearing vs. seeing, 96, 108-9

historical context, 11-12, 19, 55, 190 (*see also* persecution: first century)

original audience, 21-28

purpose of, 9, 13-16, 45, 113, 176-77, 189

repetition in, 34-43, 44-46, 54-55, 190

symbolism in, 50-55, 190

Trinitarian theology, 61-62

Roma (goddess), 28, 157

Roman Empire

as Babylon, 157, 161

blasphemy on coinage, 26-28, 135

emperor worship, 25, 27-29, 73, 86, 132, 135

as first beast, 26, 132, 133

S

sacrificial system, 97, 120

sanctification, 176

Sardis, church of, 12, 89

Satan

binding of, 172-73

casting down of, 131-32

counterfeit of divine, 133, 134, 135

defeat in last battle, 173-74

as the dragon (Rev 12), 26, 130-32, 172

as the serpent (Rev 12), 60, 130, 172

use of the beasts (Rev 13), 133-38

See also spiritual warfare

scroll (Rev 5), 96

scroll (Rev 10), 119

sealing of 144,000 (Rev 7), 108-11

seals

first through fourth, 101-4, 113

fifth, 102, 104-5, 113

sixth, 34-35, 102, 105-7, 113, 148, 149, 175

seventh, 35, 102, 112-13

relation to trumpets and bowls, 35, 112

second coming

arrival, 167

events leading to, 35-37

final battle, 168-70

like a thief in the night, 150, 152

seed (Gen 3:15, Rev 12), 60, 130

sēmainō (sign), 51-52

seraphim, 93

serpent (Gen 3, Rev 12), 60, 130, 172

seven, 77, 81, 159

seven churches of Revelation, 83-84

as all churches, 81-82

T

V

Scripture Index

Old Testament

New Testament